SECOND EDITION

tiny campsites

Discover Britain's little pockets of camping bliss

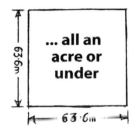

... all an acre or under

63·6m

63·6m

Dixe Wills

Tiny Campsites (2nd edition)
This edition published in the UK in 2012 by
Punk Publishing Ltd
3 The Yard
Pegasus Place
London
SE11 5SD

www.punkpublishing.co.uk

A catalogue record of this book is available from the British Library.

ISBN 978-1-906889-54-8

10 9 8 7 6 5 4 3 2 1

For Carl, who taught me everything
I know about camping.

And for Mike, who didn't.

Contents

Introduction

'Man is small and, therefore, small is beautiful.'

That's how I began the introduction to the first edition of *Tiny Campsites* and, two years later, the late philosopher-economist EF Schumacher's words continue to hold considerable amounts of water. Certainly, when it comes to campsites, the evidence backing his assertion remains irresistible: whether on a farm, by the sea, behind a pub, beside a river, on a tiny island or even next to a museum, a small campsite will always triumph over a large one, as a boutique will prevail over a chain store. It's a matter of soul.

So, what's new in the second edition of the nation's favourite guide to bijou camping grounds? More than I expected, to tell you the truth. No fewer than nine of the 75 sites in the first edition have bitten the dust for a variety of reasons, none of which has anything to do with a lack of popularity. A further campsite closed its museum, while another moved across Lincolnshire (happily, it's now even nicer than before – see p90).

Thankfully, I've unearthed a host of inspiring campsites, some of them brand new, to replace those that have gone from growing daisies to pushing them up. Among them comes a tiny slew attached to hostels. Not only are these in stonking locations, but the hostel facilities are open to campers, so if it pours with rain, there's every chance of a consoling fire and a Scrabble board nearby. Among other fresh entries there's an isle-based campsite (p172), a new site slap-bang on Hadrian's Wall (p130) and somewhere you can learn to meditate, become proficient in bushcraft or even kickbox, depending on whether you fancy inner healing, a closer walk with nature, or a little violence (p156).

Since the world insists on whirling on its axis, the info sections for every campsite in the book have been fully updated. So, if that terrific pub just down the road now does Sunday lunches, you'll read about it here. Probably first, unless you've been keeping tabs on it independently.

Anyway, I expect you're wondering how I came to write this book in the first place. (It's a more interesting story than you might imagine, if only mildly.) In 2001 I'd enjoyed a very pleasant day cycling around Dartmoor and, with evening drawing in, I made for a campsite marked on my OS map. Hauling myself over one last hill, the trees parted and I looked down on the slice of Devon that was to be my home for the night. But at the sight of it my heart sank. The bijou glade of my imaginings was, in reality, a huge commercial site that seemed to have been styled after a particularly unfortunate internment camp – rows of statics and expanses of tarmac. At the bottom of the hill I took out my map: no other campsites for miles.

I was just resigning myself to my fate when a handwritten 'Camping' sign caught my eye. Minutes later I was putting my tent up on the lawn of a gorgeous farmhouse. Birds flitted around me, an apple tree proffered free pudding and my pitch was ringed on three sides by flowerbeds bursting with colour – it was heaven. And still is, in fact – it's Sweet Meadows (p34).

I spend a great deal of my time wandering around Britain (it's okay, I'm a travel writer, it's what we do) and for two or three months a year I'm under canvas, so I've stumbled across a good number of tiny campsites over the years. But when I started looking for a book on the nation's best diminutive campsites it became apparent that if I wanted one I would have to write it myself. And so it was that I ended up cycling over 2,000 miles in a (let's face it, highly enjoyable) bid to winkle out the finest campsites in Britain of an acre or under. Also included is the useful information most camping books leave out: nearby pub and shop opening hours and what coins you might need for the showers. After all, there's nothing like arriving at a remote site hungry and foodless because you didn't know that Wednesday was early closing, or finding yourself stripped and ready for action only to discover that you haven't a single 20p piece to your name.

Anyway, since you're probably only reading this introduction if you're at a campsite and haven't brought along another book, I shall end here – first, by hoping you derive as much pleasure from visiting these sites as I have, and then by reminding you that if you're at any of the places on pages 68, 140, 152, 160 or 178, you're in luck – they've all got little libraries.

How to Use this Book

Campsite tariffs – an enigma for our times

Visit a dozen campsites and the likelihood is that they'll have 12 different ways of charging customers. Some quote a price per person; others per unit; still others per pitch, while some employ arcane algebraic formulae where x = *the cubic volume of the tent multiplied by π, and y = the number of campers divided by the square root of their IQ.* Then there are discounts for children, for those arriving by public transport; extra charges for dogs, cars, awnings and electric hook-ups; the list goes on… So, to simplify matters, in this book the cost of each campsite is given in £ signs to indicate roughly what you can expect to pay if you are:

• A solo backpacker/cyclist (BP) with a small tent
• A couple: two people sharing a medium-sized tent
• A family: two adults and two children sharing a large tent

£	=	Up to £5
££	=	Up to £10
£££	=	Up to £15
££££	=	Up to £20
£££££	=	Over £20

So, if the cost at Happy Clappy Farm is quoted as: BP £, Couple ££, Family ££££, it means that a backpacker would normally pay less than £5; a couple would fork out somewhere between a fiver and a tenner between them; while a family would be charged £15 to £20. Please note, however, that at some campsites, campervanners and caravanners may pay extra, especially if they want some electricity too.

All the campsites in this book supply free drinking water, usually from a conveniently placed standpipe.

Symbols

![tents icon] tents	![VW icon] vintage VW campervans only
![campervan icon] all campervans	![caravan icon] caravans

Tiny Campsites' Rating		Friendliness	
✳	Great	☺	Welcoming
✳✳	Fantastic	☺ ☺	Highly convivial
✳✳✳	Drop dead gorgeous	☺ ☺ ☺	Chums for life

Out and About recommendations are, as a general rule, listed in order of the author's (admittedly subjective) preference.

Key to abbreviations:

FACILITIES	OUT AND ABOUT
4U = 4 unisex toilets/showers	7D = 7 days a week
1M = 1 men's toilet/shower	U14 = under the age of 14
2W = 2 ladies' toilets/showers	News-tob-con = newsagent-tobacconist-confectioner
1D = 1 disabled toilet/shower	
CDP = chemical disposal point	PO = post office
4WD = 4-wheel-drive vehicle	w/e = weekend
max. = maximum of	BH = Bank Holiday
min. = minutes	pp = per person
	NT site = National Trust website, www.nationaltrust.org.uk

Top Tips

Help! What should I pack?

If you're new to camping and live in mortal fear of turning up at some remote campsite having forgotten a vital item of equipment, then panic no more. Aside from a tent, sleeping bag and mat, spare clothes (including waterproofs) and toiletries, these are the essentials to pop in your rucksack:

- cooking equipment (stove, fuel, lighter, pan, cutlery, mug, bowl)
- food (couscous is brilliant – avoid tins and anything overly ambitious)
- tea bags (it's not camping otherwise)
- tools (Swiss Army knife, head torch, map and compass)
- frisbee (entertainment and plate rolled into one)
- milk powder (great when far from supplies of fresh milk)
- loo roll (handy emergency pillow, among other uses)
- water bottle
- basic first aid kit

Camping is about being free and easy, so try not to pack the kitchen sink (if you really need one, you can fashion one out of twigs when you get there).

Pitching your tent

Everyone who's been camping for any length of time has a camping disaster story to tell: a tent that leaked, a tent that got washed away, a tent that got blown away or a tent that defied all attempts to be erected in the first place. However, there's no reason why any of these calamities should necessarily befall you. If you follow a few simple rules, you may never find

yourself fighting with a guy rope in the pouring rain at two o'clock in the morning. Unless, of course, that's what you like to do.

- Always have a practice go at putting up a new tent before you travel to check that you can do it and all its parts are included.
- It may seem like stating the obvious, but do read the instructions carefully while pitching your tent. Following your instincts rather than the little pictures on the stuff sack may be more fun at first but is a course of action that is likely to end badly, if not in tears.
- In blustery weather, pitch your tent with its smaller end directly into the wind. Use all the guy ropes available, and weigh each peg down with a large stone (or similar) to anchor it.
- Insert pegs so they point outwards from the tent at roughly 45 degrees.
- Don't let anything inside your tent push the inner compartment on to the flysheet as this will let water into the tent.
- Keep your tent ventilated to avoid condensation building up inside.

Midges

The Biting Midge, a member of the mighty *Ceratopogonidae* family, is not only the summer curse of the Scottish Highlands, but often makes its way south as far as northern England. However, if you forget to pack the anti-midge lotion or fail to eat Marmite every day for a fortnight beforehand (yes, it works – no pest enjoys supping Marmite-tainted blood), don't worry, as there are still plenty of ways to keep yourself bite-free.

- Wear white or light-coloured clothing
- Stay in the sun rather than shade.
- Avoid sitting outside in the early morning or late evening.
- Get yourself into a breeze or create your own by keeping on the move.

Top Five

1 **Broad Meadow House** p26

A breathtaking vista of the Cornish coast, a picturesque village and harbour to explore, a maximum of 12 campers on site and a scrummy breakfast brought to your tent each morning. Absolute heaven.

2 **Park Farm** p122

Think of the finest view of the countryside imaginable and then double it. Double it again and you've got the view from Park Farm. That's a cool 50 miles to Tan Hill and the Yorkshire Dales, and everything in between is one generous dollop of gorgeous English countryside. Pack your watercolours.

3 **Middle Ninfa Farm** p142

Consider Middle Ninfa, with its private pitches high up on the edge of the Brecon Beacons, as your very own Welsh bolt-hole. And should you ever tire of the panoramic view you can always avail yourself of the croquet lawn.

4 **The Lazy Duck** p174

Not so much a campsite as the best back garden you've ever spent the night in. There's room for just four tents in this miniature Highland glade – the rest is taken up by hammocks, red squirrels and, yes, loads of lazy ducks...

5 **Badrallach** p178

Tucked beneath a mountain on the north-west coast of Scotland, Badrallach makes other off-the-beaten-track campsites look positively urban. Bring your sea legs too: there are kayaks for hire and a loch waiting to be explored.

Campsites Sorted

The easy way to choose your site

TENTS ONLY

- No 1 Land's End
- 4 Dennis Farm
- 10 California Cottage
- 14 Daneway Inn
- 15 Abbey Home Farm
- 17 Rushey Lock
- 18 Pinkhill Lock
- 19 Cookham Lock
- 20 Gumber Farm
- 21 Evergreen Farm
- 23 Welsummer
- 26 The Jolly Sailor
- 29 Scaldbeck Cottage
- 40 Piel Island
- 43 Jelley Legs
- 46 Park Farm
- 50 Quarryside
- 53 Lone Wolf
- 54 Llanddeusant
- 55 Middle Ninfa Farm
- 59 Five Saints
- 62 Buzzard Rock
- 68 Blinkbonny Wood
- 69 Inchcailloch
- 70 The Lazy Duck

KIDS

- 1 Land's End
- 2 Coverack
- 4 Dennis Farm
- 6 Little Wenfork
- 15 Abbey Home Farm
- 21 Evergreen Farm
- 25 Spencer's Farm Shop
- 31 The Bubble Car Museum
- 33 Nicholson Farm
- 41 Birchbank Farm
- 42 Dalegarth
- 45 Wold Farm
- 52 Eastern Slade Farm
- 54 Llanddeusant
- 55 Middle Ninfa Farm
- 59 Five Saints
- 60 Ty'n Cornel

- 63 Gwersyll Maes-y-Bryn
- 65 Treheli Farm
- 68 Blinkbonny Wood

WALKERS

- 1 Land's End
- 2 Coverack
- 3 Broad Meadow House
- 7 Sweet Meadows
- 8 Millslade
- 10 California Cottage
- 12 Church Farm
- 13 Rectory Farm
- 17 Rushey Lock
- 18 Pinkhill Lock
- 19 Cookham Lock
- 20 Gumber Farm
- 21 Evergreen Farm
- 28 Potton Hall
- 29 Scaldbeck Cottage
- 30 Braham Farm
- 34 The Buzzards
- 37 The Wild Boar Inn
- 38 Rowan Bank
- 39 Crawshaw Farm
- 41 Birchbank Farm
- 42 Dalegarth
- 44 Elmtree Farm
- 45 Wold Farm
- 46 Park Farm
- 47 Highside Farm
- 48 The Old Vicarage
- 49 Rye Hill Farm
- 50 Quarryside
- 51 Porthllisky Farm
- 54 Llanddeusant
- 55 Middle Ninfa Farm
- 56 The Castle Inn
- 57 Radnors End
- 59 Five Saints
- 60 Ty'n Cornel
- 61 Ty Maen
- 62 Buzzard Rock
- 64 Silver Birches
- 65 Treheli Farm
- 68 Blinkbonny Wood
- 69 Inchcailloch

- 70 The Lazy Duck
- 72 Badrallach

CYCLISTS

- 4 Dennis Farm
- 9 Bridge Farm
- 12 Church Farm
- 16 Lyneham Lake
- 21 Evergreen Farm
- 31 The Bubble Car Museum
- 33 Nicholson Farm
- 34 The Buzzards
- 37 The Wild Boar Inn
- 39 Crawshaw Farm
- 43 Jelley Legs
- 44 Elmtree Farm
- 46 Park Farm
- 48 The Old Vicarage
- 50 Quarryside
- 56 The Castle Inn
- 57 Radnors End
- 59 Five Saints
- 62 Buzzard Rock
- 66 The Ken Bridge Hotel
- 67 Glenmidge Smiddy
- 70 The Lazy Duck

WILD

- 14 Daneway Inn
- 15 Abbey Home Farm
- 21 Evergreen Farm
- 23 Welsummer
- 24 Woodland Farm
- 40 Piel Island
- 53 Lone Wolf
- 55 Middle Ninfa Farm
- 62 Buzzard Rock
- 68 Blinkbonny
- 69 Inchcailloch

PUBS

- 11 P
- 14

37 The Wild Boar Inn
40 Piel Island
56 The Castle Inn
66 The Ken Bridge Hotel
74 Halladale Inn

COASTAL

1   Land's End
2   Coverack
3   Broad Meadow House
4   Dennis Farm
10 California Cottage
26 The Jolly Sailor
29 Scaldbeck Cottage
40 Piel Island
44 Elmtree Farm
51 Porthllisky Farm
52 Eastern Slade Farm
65 Treheli Farm
72 Badrallach
73 Inver
74 Halladale Inn
75 Eilean Fraoich

WATERSIDE

4   Dennis Farm
8   Millslade
16 Lyneham Lake
17 Rushey Lock
18 Pinkhill Lock
19 Cookham Lock
32 The Green Man
36 Four Oaks
40 Piel Island
41 Birchbank Farm
42 Dalegarth
53 Lone Wolf
58 Trericket Mill
59 Five Saints
66 The Ken Bridge Hotel
69 Inchcailloch
70 The Lazy Duck
71 The Wee Camp Site
72 Badrallach

CAMPFIRES

6   Little Wenfork
7   Sweet Meadows
8   Millslade
10 California Cottage
15 Abbey Home Farm

18 Pinkhill Lock
20 Gumber Farm
21 Evergreen Farm
23 Welsummer
24 Woodland Farm
25 Spencer's Farm Shop
29 Scaldbeck Cottage
31 The Bubble Car Museum
33 Nicholson Farm
34 The Buzzards
36 Four Oaks
43 Jelley Legs
52 Eastern Slade Farm
53 Lone Wolf
54 Llanddeusant
55 Middle Ninfa Farm
58 Trericket Mill
59 Five Saints
62 Buzzard Rock
68 Blinkbonny Wood
72 Badrallach

EASY PUBLIC TRANSPORT

4   Dennis Farm
16 Lyneham Lake
25 Spencer's Farm Shop
29 Scaldbeck Cottage
32 The Green Man
34 The Buzzards
46 Park Farm
61 Ty Maen

HIDEAWAY

7   Sweet Meadows
15 Abbey Home Farm
20 Gumber Farm
21 Evergreen Farm
27 High House Fruit Farm
28 Potton Hall
34 The Buzzards
36 Four Oaks
39 Crawshaw Farm
41 Birchbank Farm
45 Wold Farm
46 Park Farm
47 Highside Farm
55 Middle Ninfa Farm
59 Five Saints
60 Ty'n Cornel
62 Buzzard Rock

64 Silver Birches
68 Blinkbonny Wood
69 Inchcailloch

VIEWS

1   Land's End
3   Broad Meadow House
4   Dennis Farm
5   Scadghill Farm
6   Little Wenfork
9   Bridge Farm
12 Church Farm
30 Braham Farm
35 Forestside Farm
37 The Wild Boar Inn
38 Rowan Bank
39 Crawshaw Farm
40 Piel Island
46 Park Farm
47 Highside Farm
51 Porthllisky Farm
52 Eastern Slade Farm
54 Llanddeusant
55 Middle Ninfa Farm
57 Radnors End
62 Buzzard Rock
65 Treheli Farm
69 Inchcailloch
71 The Wee Camp Site
72 Badrallach
73 Inver
74 Halladale Inn

WATER SPORTS

2   Coverack
3   Broad Meadow House
4   Dennis Farm
5   Scadghill Farm
10 California Cottage
17 Rushey Lock
18 Pinkhill Lock
19 Cookham Lock
22 Cedar Gables
26 The Jolly Sailor
29 Scaldbeck Cottage
32 The Green Man
57 Radnors End
58 Trericket Mill
66 The Ken Bridge Hotel
69 Inchcailloch
72 Badrallach
74 Halladale Inn

South-West England

1 Land's End
2 Coverack
3 Broad Meadow House
4 Dennis Farm
5 Scadghill Farm
6 Little Wenfork
7 Sweet Meadows
8 Millslade
9 Bridge Farm

Letcha Vean
St Just-in-Penwith
Penzance
Cornwall
TR19 7NT

Chris Nelson
01736 788437
landsend@yha.org.uk
www.yha.org.uk
Landranger: 203 (SW 364 305)

THE BASICS
Size: ½ acre.
Pitches: 20 people (0 hardstanding).
Terrain: Grassy – some flat and some slightly slopey pitches.
Shelter: On all sides except seaward, where there's some bracken and shrubs to hide behind.
View: The sea at Porth Nanven and Cape Cornwall.
Waterside: No.
Electric hook-ups: No.
Noise/Light/Olfactory pollution: Lights from hostel in evening.

THE FACILITIES
Loos: 6U. **Showers**: 6U (free).
Other facilities: Cycle store, dining room, lounge, kitchenette and kitchen, drying room; wine and bottled beer for sale; hostel meals available. Maps at reception.
Stuff for children: Board games.
Recycling: Everything (inc. compost).

THE RULES
Dogs: Yes (but not allowed in hostel).
Fires: No open fires but BBQ provided.
Other: Reception open 8–10am & 5–11pm.

PUB LIFE
The King's Arms (St Austell brewery), St Just (1 mile) – inn built in the 14th century to accommodate the builders of the church next door; open 12–'late' 7D; food served Mon–Sat 12–2.30pm (till 2pm in winter) & 6–9pm (5–8pm in winter), Sun 12–4pm (booking strongly advised in evening); quiz nights Wednesday 9pm; 01736 788545; bit.ly/sCPagb.

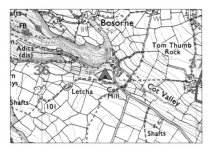

SHOP
Co-op, St Just (1 mile) – small supermarket; open 8am–10pm 7D; 01736 788728. St Just has some good independent shops.

THERE AND AWAY
Train station: Penzance (9 miles) – London to Penzance line. Take the twice-daily bus no. 504 (www.westerngreyhound.com) to Kelynack, a little under a mile from the site.

OUT AND ABOUT
South West Coast Path (0.3 miles) – amble down a footpath for 5 minutes and you're on it. Head south for lovely Sennen Cove (3½ miles) or north for the abandoned tin mine at Zawn a Bal (2½ miles), as fêted in *The Z–Z of Great Britain*; www.southwestcoastpath.com.
Minack Theatre (8½ miles) – if the play (season May to September) doesn't grab you at this cliffside open-air theatre, there's the Atlantic to gaze upon; daytime visit: adult £4, child (12–15) £2, U12 free; open April to September 9.30am–5.30pm (shorter hours the rest of the year) 7D; 01736 810181; www.minack.com.

open	Mid July to end August
tiny campsites' rating	★ ★ ★
friendliness	☺ ☺
cost	BP £££ Couple £££££ Family £££££

The youth hostel at Land's End is not, strictly speaking, at Land's End but several miles to the north-east. However, given the money-grubbing monument to tackiness that Land's End has become, this can be counted as something of a blessing. Thus, instead of the Cornish Pantry and the West Country Shopping Village, you'll be greeted with a view down a narrow valley to the sea. Lovers of greens and blues should apply here, for the scene is unblemished by human hand but for an obelisk high on Cape Cornwall and a scattering of picturesque houses.

Filling the hostel's back lawn, the campsite is a peculiar but not unsatisfying mixture of wild camping (its boundaries are set by bracken and bramble, and numerous rabbits come to visit) and mild camping (you're never more than 30 seconds from the hostel's wine list). There's a tiny campers' kitchenette in an annex and a much larger and better equipped kitchen in the hostel itself. Generously, all the hostel facilities (including a lounge where board games are often cracked open of an evening) are available to those using the campsite, so, if you've forgotten your stove or like to dine *a table*, you're well catered for (even if you're doing the catering yourself).

St Just, the patron saint of Having Enough But No More, has also given his name to the nearest village. Should you yearn for civilisation, a 20-minute walk will take you to its art galleries and Plen an Gwarry, a medieval open-air performance area that takes centre stage on Lafrowda Day, the village's annual festival of arts and music (third Sat in July).

Parc Behan
School Hill
Coverack
Helston
Cornwall
TR12 6SA

Phil Bedford
01326 280687
coverack@yha.org.uk
www.yha.org.uk
Landranger: 204 (SW 782 181)

THE BASICS
Size: ¼ acre.
Pitches: Max. 30 people (0 hardstanding).
Terrain: Some flat pitches, most slightly sloping.
Shelter: Yes, from all sides.
View: Perprean Cove and The Oxen (large rocks out to sea).
Waterside: No.
Electric hook-ups: No.
Noise/Light/Olfactory pollution: Next to a minor road, but traffic light at night; lights from hostel buildings and the street.

THE FACILITIES
Loos: 5U 1W. **Showers**: 5U 1W (free).
Other facilities: Campers' kitchen: oven and hob, 2 larder fridges, washing machine (£2.50; detergent 75p), washing-up, a kettle and toaster. Use of larger hostel kitchen, lounge, dining room, conservatory, drying room, cycle store and pool table. Breakfast (£4.95), dinner (£7.50; always 1 veggie dish, vegan if pre-booked), packed lunch (£5.50).
Stuff for children: Badminton sets, bodyboards, buckets and spades. Also, 'Wildlife Explorer Kits' (free, £10 deposit) – bumbags filled with handy equipment.
Recycling: Everything (inc. compost).

THE RULES
Dogs: No. **Fires**: Yes, off grass.
Other: No massive tents.

PUB LIFE
The Paris Hotel (St Austell brewery), Coverack (200 metres); open 'roughly' 11.30am–midnight (noon–11pm in winter); breakfast 8–9am; lunch noon–2.30pm; dinner 5.30–9.30pm (6–8.30pm

in winter); quiz nights Wednesday 9pm; 01326 280258; www.pariscoverack.com.

SHOP
Brenda's, Coverack (275 metres) – basic victuals (and a free-to-use cash machine); Mon–Sat 8am–6pm, Sun 8am–5.30pm; 01326 280401. The hostel sells a range of wines, local beers, non-alcoholic drinks, soap and toothbrushes.

THERE AND AWAY
Train station: Penmere (11½ miles via the Helford Ferry) – Truro to Falmouth line. Or from Penryn station take bus no. 2 to Helston then no. 538 to Coverack.

OUT AND ABOUT
National Seal Sanctuary, Gweek (9¼ miles) – otters and penguins too – open 7 days a *gweek* from 10am; 08714 232110; www.sealsanctuary.co.uk.
Roskilly's Ice Cream Farm (2½ miles) – delicious organic dairy farm; free; milking at 4.30–5pm(ish), café open Sun–Wed 9am–6pm, Thur–Sat 9am–9pm; 01326 280479; www.roskillys.co.uk.

open	March to November
tiny campsites' rating	★ ★ ★
friendliness	☺ ☺
cost	BP ££, Couple ££££, Family £££££

It is the road, twisting like a panicked snake escaping up the hill from Coverack's harbour, that has imprinted itself on the minds of generations of holidaying children, leaving the ice lollies and the boat rides to slip unnoticed from memory's grasp. Near the top, lording it over the bay, stands a white-painted youth hostel defying the sea gales to strike its foursquare features. And beside the hostel, tucked neatly behind thick hedges laced with ivy and brambles, sits the campsite.

In fact, it's tempting to say there are actually three campsites here, for there's a trio of grassy areas on which to pitch, each with its own separate identity. The first, by the hostel, is flat and enjoys a (slightly restricted) sea view. Its neighbour is an apple orchard (come in late summer and slip the eaters and cookers into picnics and puddings). While what was once a walled kitchen garden off the orchard offers two or three lucky owners of small tents their own private and secluded little world.

As for facilities, these are about as good as you're ever going to get at a campsite. Both the swish modern shower and loo block and the campers' kitchen are kept absolutely spotless.

In other news, we have Noel and Winnow Hardy to thank for the fact that there is a campsite here at all. The orchard was going to be sold off for development in 1993 but the Hardys intervened, recruiting local people in a successful campaign to save it. Noel and Winnow, a tiny camping nation salutes you.

Broad Meadow House

Quay Road
Charlestown
St Austell
Cornwall
PL25 3NX

Deb Best
01726 76636
stay@broadmeadowhouse.com
www.broadmeadowhouse.com
Landranger: 200 (SX 040 516)

THE BASICS
Size: ⅖ acre.
Pitches: Max. 12 people on site (0 hardstanding).
Terrain: Slopey, but all pitches level.
Shelter: From all sides but seaward.
View: The shoreline of St Austell Bay.
Waterside: Cliffs 100 metres.
Electric hook-ups: 4.
Noise/Light/Olfactory pollution: None.

THE FACILITIES
Loos: 1U. **Showers**: 1U (free).
Other facilities: Washing-up sink, mini fridge & freezer, wi-fi, recharging point.
Stuff for children: A separate field for games.
Recycling: Everything.

THE RULES
Dogs: If well behaved and on leads. Max. 2 per party. **Fires**: No open fires; BBQs off grass (granite blocks available).
Other: Only campervans accepted are small vintage VW vans.

PUB LIFE
Pier House Hotel (free house), Charlestown (200 metres) – harbourside snug bar with highly recommended food and live entertainment Sat evenings; bar open Mon–Thur 11am–11pm, Fri–Sat till midnight, Sun 12–11pm; food served 8–11am & 12–9.30pm 7D; 01726 67955; www.pierhousehotel.com.

SHOP
Carlyon Bay PO (1 mile via coastal path) – quite basic supplies; open Mon–Fri 7am–5.30pm, Sat till 5pm, Sun 8am–12.30pm;

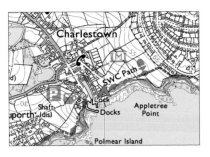

01726 812728. The mobile 'Orange Shop' appears on the Charlestown Quay daily from 10am to 5pm to supply delicious locally grown food and artisan bread.

THERE AND AWAY
Train station: St Austell (1½ miles) – Plymouth to Penzance line. The Western Greyhound bus no. 525 runs hourly from St Austell to Charlestown.

OUT AND ABOUT
Charlestown Shipwreck & Heritage Centre (50 metres) – 'the largest collection of shipwreck artefacts in Britain'; adult £5.95, 10–16 £2.95, U10 free; open daily March to October 10am–5pm; 01726 69897; www.shipwreckcharlestown.com.
Eden Project, Bodelva (4 miles – footpath route maps from campsite available) – each football-like biome takes you into a different region in the world, and there are large discounts if you arrive by foot or bicycle (see website for prices); open daily April to October 9am (ticket desks open at 9.30am), various closing times; 01726 811911; www.edenproject.com.

open	May to September (weather dependent)
tiny campsites' rating	✴ ✴ ✴
friendliness	☺ ☺ ☺
cost	BP ££, Couple ££££, Family £££££

Walk past Charlestown's museum and along the short cul-de-sac behind it and you'd be forgiven for being sceptical about there being a campsite here at all, let alone one of the tastiest in the country. However, just beyond the final house, a gate opens up to a couple of tiny fields that command fabulous views out to sea and along the shoreline towards Black Head, the tip of a headland sporting the golden flash of a wheat field on its back.

Broad Meadow (Was it ever broad? Ancient sepia photos suggest not.) has two geese, one furnished and flashy Karsten tent (£30/adult for 'tent and breakfast') and plenty of space for people who'd rather bring their own. Since the owners limit the number of campers on site to a mere dozen, you get the distinct feeling of being one of an incredibly privileged few. This is especially true if you order a delicious breakfast basket (and fresh smoothie) to be brought to your tent.

Basking sharks and grey seals are sometimes spotted in the bay (just ask to borrow the telescope) while peregrine falcons, sparrowhawks and buzzards contest the air space above. Swallows, sensibly, prefer to skim the surface of the field and are so used to company that they come quite close to feed.

In tiny Charlestown there's some easy coasteering to be had; a gig club (www.charlestown.org.uk) that allows beginners to have a go at rowing on novice nights; and, for those who want to go it alone, sea kayaks and other water vessels can be hired (www.charlestownwatersports.com).

Dennis Lane
Padstow
Cornwall
PL28 8DR

Harry and Rebecca Smith
01841 534925
www.wix.com/dennisfarm/campsite
OS Landranger: 200 (SW 920 743)

THE BASICS
Size: ⅗ acre.
Pitches: 24 (0 hardstanding).
Terrain: Sloping with some level pitches.
Shelter: On 2 sides.
View: Across the Camel Estuary to the village of Rock.
Waterside: Yes.
Electric hook-ups: No.
Noise/Light/Olfactory pollution: The globular yellow blobs of the Padstow streetlights; the salty tang of seaweed at low tide.

THE FACILITIES
Loos: 3M 4W. **Showers**: 2U & 1 disabled/family (40p tokens 'for 5 min.').
Other facilities: Washing machine, tumble-dryer, 3 washing-up areas, external shower for surfers, CDP; gas bottles for sale; ice blocks can be hired for 40p.
Stuff for children: Field for games.
Recycling: No.

THE RULES
Dogs: On leads. **Fires**: No open fires; concrete blocks available for BBQs.
Other: No large groups.

PUB LIFE
Golden Lion (free house), Lanadwell Street, Padstow (¾ mile) – dating back to the 14th century and possessor of the 'Obby 'Oss that is paraded through town every May Day to the accompaniment of drums and accordions; open 11am–11pm 7D; food served Mon–Sat 12–2.30pm & 6.30–9pm, Sun 12–2pm & 6.30–9pm; 01841 532797; www.goldenlionpadstow.co.uk.

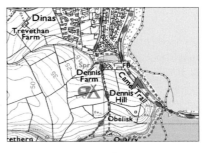

Or try the **Old Ship Hotel** (free house), Mill Square, Padstow (¾ mile) – a pub that does breakfasts if you've forgotten to pack your muesli; open 9am–11pm 7D; breakfast served 9–11am, lunch/dinner 12–9pm; 01841 532357; www.oldshiphotel-padstow.co.uk.

SHOP
Spar, Middle Street, Padstow (¾ mile) – basics and off licence; open Mon–Sat 7am–8pm, Sun 8am–7pm; 01841 533400. There's a wide range of shops in town too.

THERE AND AWAY
Train station: Bodmin Parkway (19 miles) – Exeter to Penzance line. There is a regular bus route between the station and Padstow – see main text.

OUT AND ABOUT
Camel Trail – see main text; free; always open; 01872 327310 (for free leaflet); www.sustrans.org.uk.
Padstow – there's more to the picturesque working port than the Rick Stein restaurant; www.padstowlive.com.

open	Whitsun Bank Holiday to mid September
tiny campsites' rating	✳ ✳ ✳
friendliness	☺ ☺
cost	BP £££, Couple £££££, Family £££££

The first thing you learn when staying at Dennis Farm is that it's not the campsite called Dennis Cove. The two were once one, but have now split, with the much larger Dennis Cove on one side of the headland, and the diminutive Dennis Farm site – an isolated strip of coastal loveliness, free from crowds, madding or otherwise – on the other

The view across the Camel Estuary, with its bobbing flotsam of yachts, canoes, power boats, windsurfers and water-skiers, is as eye pleasing and summery as a vista can be. The very best vantage points are at the far end of the site on a tiny plateau reserved for backpackers and cyclists.

The Camel Trail runs right through the site – you cross it to get to the smart loo block – taking cyclists, walkers and the occasional horse rider to Padstow (½ mile) or, in the other direction, to Bodmin (10½ miles) via Wadebridge (4½ miles). The trail runs along a disused railway line, making it very flat and thus a hit with young families.

All manner of bicycles, including tandems, can be hired very reasonably at Padstow Cycle Hire (www. padstowcyclehire.com).

Unusually (perhaps even uniquely), the campsite has four moorings and a slipway that can handle anything from small dinghies to 14-footers. If you'd rather arrive by land, however, bus no. 555 runs direct from Bodmin Parkway station to Padstow (www. westerngreyhound.com).

Bude
Cornwall
EX23 9HN

Jan Beak
01288 354357
OS Landranger: 190 (SS 222 102)

Size: ⅓ acre.
Pitches: 5 caravans and/or 8 tents (0 hardstanding).
Terrain: Very gently sloping.
Shelter: Hedge to east and north.
View: Dartmoor, Bodmin Moor.
Waterside: No.
Electric hook-ups: No.
Noise/Light/Olfactory pollution: Mooing.

Loos: 1U. **Showers**: 1U (2 x 10p for '6 min.').
Other facilities: CDP.
Stuff for children: No.
Recycling: Everything.

Dogs: On leads. **Fires**: No open fires; BBQs off grass. **Other**: No.

New Inn (free house), Kilkhampton (2½ miles) – a 15th-century pub with its own skittle alley (available September to May); open Mon–Fri 11am–3pm & 6–11pm, Sat 11am–11pm, Sun 12–10.30pm; food served 12–2pm & 6–9pm 7D; 01288 321488; www.newinncornwall.com.

Kilkhampton (2½ miles) runs to a **Premier** (convenience store; 8am–8pm 7D) and a **Spar** (convenience store and off licence; 8am–8pm 7D) as well as a fish-and-chip shop, a pizzeria, a PO and a toy shop.

Train station: Gunnislake (34 miles) – Gunnislake to Plymouth line. If you

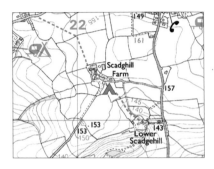

enjoy a bus marathon, take bus no. 79 to Callington, no. 576 to Bude, then no. 530 to Stibb, from where it's a 10-minute walk.

Bude (3½ miles) – a curious place: a seaside town that revolves around its river and canal, and yet has made its name as a surfers' paradise. If you'd rather swim, head for the sea pool at Summerleaze Beach; www.visitbude.info.
Sandymouth Bay (1½ miles) a pleasant half-hour walk across fields and down a lane will take you to the National Trust-owned Sandymouth Bay, with its waterfalls (when enough rain has fallen), saffron beach and wild rock formations.

open	All year
tiny campsites' rating	★ ★
friendliness	☺ ☺ ☺
cost	BP ££, Couple ££, Family ££

Climb the hill from Bude up to Scadghill Farm under your own steam and it really whets your appetite for the view at the top. The panorama does not disappoint, laying before the eyes a feast of countryside spread out like a spectacularly wrinkled green tea-towel. Best of all, and high above everything else, stand what appear to be two hills. One turns out to be Bodmin Moor, some 20 miles away, while the other is Dartmoor, 25 miles to the south-east. It's difficult to believe that the former actually covers 100 square-miles, while the latter extends to a full 368; from Scadghill you feel you could scale them in one or two bounds, before breakfast if necessary.

The campsite is situated a quarter of a mile from the road, along a farm track, thus ensuring that there is nothing to disturb the peace and quiet but the low moomuring of cows. The facilities, meanwhile, can be found around the back of a nearby bungalow.

Bude will always be the number one attraction for campers here, with its renowned annual jazz festival (www.budejazzfestival.co.uk), castle turned heritage centre (bit.ly/vlQ9cf) championing Sir Goldsworthy Gurney and coastal look-out based on Athens' Temple of the Winds (every home should have one). However, both the car-free historic fishing village of Clovelly (14 miles; www.clovelly.co.uk) and Hartland Point's stunning sea views (15 miles; www.hartlandpeninsula.co.uk) are also within striking distance, and well worth the journey.

Rezare
Launceston
Cornwall
PL15 9NU

Mike and Sam Wing
01579 370755
info@littlewenfork.co.uk
www.littlewenfork.co.uk
OS Landranger: 201 (SX 354 774)

THE BASICS
Size: ½ acre.
Pitches: 5 (2 hardstanding). Max. 12 people on site.
Terrain: Slightly sloping.
Shelter: Hedge shelters from east and west.
View: Kit Hill.
Waterside: No.
Electric hook-ups: No.
Noise/Light/Olfactory pollution: No.

THE FACILITIES
Loos: 1U. **Showers**: 1U (free).
Other facilities: Indoor and outdoor washing-up areas, iceblock freezing service, CDP, free-range eggs for sale.
Stuff for children: Animals to pet.
Recycling: Everything.

THE RULES
Dogs: On leads.
Fires: Platform for fire at top of field and oil drums available to use as braziers.
Other: Close the gate to keep cows out.

PUB LIFE
The Springer Spaniel (free house), Treburley (½ mile) – 18th-century pub serving locally sourced food, some of which is from its own organic farm; open Sun–Thur 12–3pm & 6–11pm, Fri & Sat till midnight; food served 12–1.45pm & 6.30–8.45pm 7D; 01579 370424; www.thespringerspaniel.org.uk.

SHOP
Stoke Climsland PO (2½ miles) – small but packed to the rafters with supplies; open Mon–Fri 7am–6pm, Sat till 12.30pm, Sun 8–11am; 01579 370201.

THERE AND AWAY
Train station: Gunnislake (13 miles) – Gunnislake to Plymouth line. Take bus no. 79 (www.daccoaches.co.uk) to Callington, then hop onto no. 576 (www.westerngreyhound.co.uk), which stops at the Springer Spaniel pub.

OUT AND ABOUT
Cotehele (9 miles) – magnificent and reputedly haunted Tudor house in large grounds; visit can be combined with a boat trip (see below); adult £9, child £4.50, family £22.50; open mid March to October, Sat–Thur 11am–4.30pm; 01579 351346; NT site.
Tree Surfers Gulworthy (9 miles) – get in touch with your inner Tarzan (or Jane) on high ropes, zip wires and a tree jump, or try out some archery or mountain biking (booking ahead essential); 01822 833409; www.treesurfers.co.uk.

open	April to October
tiny campsites' rating	✴ ✴
friendliness	☺ ☺ ☺
cost	BP ££, Couple ££, Family £££

There's a mystery surrounding Little Wenfork. This thin half-acre slip of land has divided two neighbouring farms for hundreds of years, but no one is quite sure why it's there when all the fields around it are, well, proper field size. A further layer of intrigue is supplied by the deeds, which show that in the 1800s the cigar-shaped plot was lost (and thus also won) in a bet. With regard to the how and the why of the wager, however, the documents remain stubbornly silent.

Today's owners are unlikely to hand the field over to you on the turn of a single card but, as consolation, you can enjoy a cracking view of Kit Hill and parts of the Tamar Valley, an area of outstanding natural beauty. In case you missed it in the news, the hill was given to the villagers of Callington by Prince Charles on the birth of his son William. The area is now a country park open to the public and, on a clear day, views of both the north and the south coasts of Cornwall can be seen from the top.

There are three beautifully furnished bell tents for hire while a small allotment is home to ducks, chickens and some Gloucestershire Old Spots pigs who love having their heads scratched. Children (and adults too) are at liberty to test for themselves just how great this love is. Most of the time, however, visitors are content to lie back and enjoy the wide Cornish skies that Little Wenfork, perched up on a hill, seems very close to indeed.

Clifford Bridge
Drewsteignton
Devon
EX6 6QB

📧 Mr and Mrs JR Guillebaud

☎ 01647 24331

✉ jrguillebaud@gmail.com

OS Landranger: 191 (SX 780 900)

THE BASICS
Size: ¾ acre in fields & 4 small garden pitches.
Pitches: 8 (0 hardstanding).
Terrain: Mainly flat.
Shelter: On all sides.
View: Wild wood from fields.
Waterside: Stream in woods.
Electric hook-ups: Potentially 2 (via extension leads).
Noise/Light/Olfactory pollution: No.

THE FACILITIES
Loos: 2U (one of which is a compost loo).
Showers: 1U (free).
Other facilities: No.
Stuff for children: Swing, see-saw, pony-sitting/-feeding and nature trails by arrangement.
Recycling: Glass, tins, plastic milk bottles.

THE RULES
Dogs: If well behaved (and cleaned up after). **Fires**: Yes, but only if there hasn't been a drought (please bring your own wood); BBQs off grass. **Other**: No.

PUB LIFE
Royal Oak (free house), Dunsford (2½ miles) – a country pub with numerous animals including donkeys and giant rabbits; open in summer Mon 7–9pm, Tue–Sat 12–2.30pm & 6.30–11pm, Sun 7–11pm; food served Mon 7–8pm, Tue–Sat 12–2pm & 7–9pm, Sun (if pre-booked) 7–8pm; 01647 252256; www.royaloakd.com. Or walk/cycle west along the River Teign to the **Fingle Bridge Inn** (free house), Drewsteignton (3 miles) – beer garden by the river; open in summer

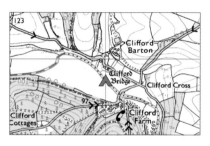

Mon–Sat 11am–10pm, Sun till 6pm; food served Mon–Sat 12–4.30pm & 6–9pm, Sun 12–3pm (daily cream teas till 5pm); 01647 281287; www.finglebridgeinn.com.

SHOP
Dunsford PO (2½ miles) – basic supplies; open Mon–Fri 8.30am–5pm (closed 1–2pm daily and Wed afternoons), Sat 9am–1pm; 01647 252330. Moretonhampstead (3 miles) has a **Co-op** and Cheriton Bishop (2½ miles) the **Chequers Store**.

THERE AND AWAY
Train station: Yeoford (6¾ miles) – Exeter to Barnstaple line (aka the Tarka line). Take a taxi from here as there's no onward bus.

OUT AND ABOUT
Castle Drogo (4½ miles) – the last castle built in England (and by Edwin Lutyens to boot); adult £8.40, child £4.20, family £21; castle open daily mid March to October 11am–5pm; 01647 433306; NT site.
Finch Foundry, Sticklepath (9¾ miles) – England's last working water-powered forge; adult £4.70, child £2.40; open daily mid March to October 11am–5pm; NT site.

open	All year
tiny campsites' rating	✹ ✹
friendliness	☺ ☺ ☺
cost	BP ££, Couple ££, Family ££

If the ultimate expression of tiny camping is to pitch your tent in someone's back garden, then Sweet Meadows, on the north-eastern edge of Dartmoor National Park, is it. Sliding past the corner of the house, you'll have to brush aside flowers competing for space in order to make it onto the back lawn with its elegant cast-iron table and chairs. There are fields for camping but, when booking, do nab a place in the garden and ask for the pitch nearest the house. Of the four lovely spaces there, this one – surrounded on three sides by flowerbeds (often blissfully overgrown and bursting with colour) and shaded by an apple tree – is so perfect you'll be hugging yourself with joy when you reach it.

Beyond, an arch in the hedge reveals a tree-swing and the wilder regions of the garden, where less clearly defined pitches take on an altogether more rustic feel. There's a paddock where the owners graze their Isle of Rum ponies and, on request, Flossie is available for kids to sit on at feeding time. Meanwhile, the shower/loo is a homely bathroom in the house, with access from the garden, and there's a posh woodland compost loo, and a shelter and hay barn should the weather turn unpleasant.

Nature lovers need only sit by their tent and wait. The site is visited by owls, three sorts of woodpecker, buzzards, sparrowhawks, swallows, hobbies, bats and badgers as well as deer. Just beyond the hedge, the woods of the Teign Valley are renowned for their daffodils and early-purple and spotted orchids, while just half a mile away there's a nature reserve at Steps Bridge.

Millslade Country House
Brendon
Lynton
Devon
EX35 6PS

Keith and Carol Cobb

☎ 01598 741322

✉ keithcarol@millslade.wanadoo.co.uk

🖵 www.millslade.co.uk

OS Landranger: 180 (SS 765 481)

THE BASICS
Size: ⅓ acre.
Pitches: 20 (0 hardstanding).
Terrain: Flat.
Shelter: All round – mainly beech and sycamore trees.
View: No.
Waterside: Yes, the East Lyn river.
Electric hook-ups: No.
Noise/Light/Olfactory pollution: The gurgle of the East Lyn.

THE FACILITIES
Loos: 2M 3W. **Showers**: No.
Other facilities: Cold water washbasins.
Stuff for children: Swing above river, adventure playground in next field.
Recycling: Everything.

THE RULES
Dogs: Under control. **Fires**: Open fires allowed (please bring your own wood); BBQs off grass or in the firepit. **Other**: No.

PUB LIFE
Staghunters Inn (free house), Brendon (200 metres) – the oldest section of the pub was Millslade Abbey's chapel before Henry VIII dissolved it. The food comes recommended and they also sell books of local walks; open 12–11.30pm 7D (April to September – times variable during rest of year); food served Mon–Sat 12–2.10pm & 6–8.30pm, Sun 12–1.50pm & 7–8.30pm; 01598 741222; www.staghunters.com.

SHOP
Costcutter, Lynton (4 miles) – large convenience store and off licence; open 7am–9pm 7D; 01598 753438.

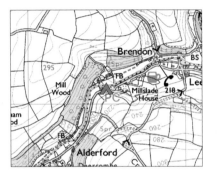

THERE AND AWAY
Train station: Barnstaple (22 miles) – Barnstaple to Exeter line (aka the Tarka line). Bus no. 310 runs between Barnstaple and Lynton.

OUT AND ABOUT
Lynmouth (3½ miles) – wonderful (if rather touristy) harbour on the precipitous River Lyn and scene of notorious floods in 1952; 0845 6603232; www.lynton-lynmouth-tourism.co.uk.
Lynton & Barnstaple Railway (6¾ miles) – despite its name, the L&BR actually runs for just a mile between Woody Bay station and Killington Lane, but its tiny steam engines have got 'happy summertime memory' written all over them (though not literally, of course); adult return £7, U15 £3, U5 free, family £18; open daily in summer, for timetable see website; 01598 763487; www.lynton-rail.co.uk.

DEVON

open	March to October
tiny campsites' rating	★ ★
friendliness	☺
cost	BP £, Couple ££, Family £££

Whether you come by car, bike or on foot, the most satisfying way to approach Brendon is by hauling yourself up onto Exmoor from Lynmouth. After scaling Countisbury Hill, an unrelenting and often quite steep climb, and catching the extraordinary view at the top (while being blown about by the inevitable gales), the descent into cosy Brendon is an unalloyed joy. The shelter this little valley settlement affords gives you the feeling of having snuggled into a comfy bed.

Breezing over the bridge that crosses the East Lyn river, once Brendon's main street, you'll find Millslade a few hundred metres to the west, marking the edge of a village that squeezes itself into the valley bottom like a line of toothpaste. This is no ordinary valley either; it is known as Hidden Valley or Lorna Doone Valley, according to taste. Malmsmead, where much of RD Blackmore's book was set, is just a couple of miles along the river.

The campsite, in common with the village, stretches itself along the East Lyn. Hedges and trees afford protection. loos come courtesy of a Portakabin, but drinking water must be collected from Millslade House, about 100 metres away.

In the local inn, the Staghunters, Doone-esque conversations can still be heard. Ask them to tell you about the rogue who, adding to his growing list of alleged petty crimes (and progeny in every village) is suspected of having killed the largest stag in the surrounding area. It's a different world all right.

West Bradley
Glastonbury
Somerset
BA6 8LU

David and Lene Cotton
01458 850431
info@bridgefarmcaravansite.co.uk
www.bridgefarmcaravansite.co.uk
Landranger: 183 (ST 552 363)

THE BASICS
Size: ⅗ acre.
Pitches: 12 (0 hardstanding). Max. 5 motorhomes per night.
Terrain: Flat.
Shelter: From all sides but north.
View: Glastonbury Tor.
Waterside: No.
Electric hook-ups: 6.
Noise/Light/Olfactory pollution: No.

THE FACILITIES
Loos: 1M 1W. **Showers**: 1U (free).
Other facilities: Washing-up area, plug for phone chargers, CDP, freezer for iceblocks.
Stuff for children: Milking time can be watched on request.
Recycling: Everything.

THE RULES
Dogs: On leads. **Fires**: No open fires; BBQs off grass. **Other**: No.

PUB LIFE
The Lion (Punch Taverns), West Pennard (2 miles) – friendly country pub with occasional morris dancing; open Mon, 6–11pm, Tues–Sun 12–3pm & 6–11pm (Sun till 10.30pm); food served Mon 6–9.15pm, Tues–Sat 12–2.15pm & 6–9.15pm, Sun 12–2.15pm; 01458 832941; www.thelionatpennard.co.uk.
The Apple Tree Inn (free house), West Pennard (2 miles) – swish pub serving locally sourced victuals; open Tues–Sat 10.30am–3pm & 6–11pm, Sun 10.30am–4pm; food served Tues–Fri 12–2pm & 6–9pm, Sat 12–2pm & 6–9.30pm, Sun 12–3pm & 6–9.30pm; 01749 890060; www.appletreeglastonbury.co.uk.

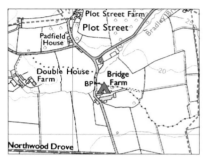

SHOP
Baltonsborough PO (1¾ miles) – basic supplies and a small off licence; open Mon–Fri 7.30am–1pm & 2–6pm, Sat 7.30am–1pm, Sun 8.30–11am; 01458 850249.

THERE AND AWAY
Train station: Castle Cary (8 miles) – London to Exeter line. Nippy Bus Ltd (www.nippybus.co.uk) runs bus no. 667 between Castle Cary and West Bradley.

OUT AND ABOUT
Glastonbury Abbey (4½ miles) – set in 36 acres of parkland, this reputed burial place of King Arthur was once Britain's largest abbey; adult £6, U16 £4, U5 free, family £16; open daily from 9am, closing time varies throughout the year; 01458 832267; www.glastonburyabbey.com.
Glastonbury Tor (3 miles) – the focal point for more myths and legends than you can shake some 'shtick' at, plus an astonishing view from the top; free; always open; 01934 844518; NT site.

open	Easter to Halloween
tiny campsites' rating	★ ★
friendliness	☺ ☺
cost	BP ££, Couple ££, Family ££

Glastonbury Tor, with the sun setting behind its simple church tower, makes for one of the great iconic views of England. It's also home to the King of the Fairies, Gwyn ap Nudd, so it's nice to know that such a regal spot can be enjoyed from an unfussy field on a farm on the Somerset Levels.

Of course, had you come here many hundreds of years ago, you could have reached the Tor by boat, possibly sailing right over Bridge Farm in the process. Legend has it that the teenage Jesus visited here with Joseph of Arimathea, an unlikely event that inspired William Blake to pen 'Jerusalem'.

The campsite on the 600-acre Bridge Farm is a simple square, bordered on three sides by hedges. Meanwhile, the generously sized loos and shower are a short walk away through an adjoining field.

The quiet, flat roads around the farm are perfect for novice cyclists or, indeed, experienced cyclists who want to take it easy. There's a National Byway Loop (www.thenationalbyway.org) very close by that uses minor roads to form a circuit taking in Glastonbury

and Wells (turn left out of the farm then left again to join it). Alternatively, you could make up your own local route, perhaps touring the many vineyards and cider orchards that strew the area.

Glastonbury itself is a relatively level and almost car-free five miles away on back roads, should you wish to experience a gong bath or a Tibetan eye-reading, or merely need to take your crystals in for a service.

South-Central England

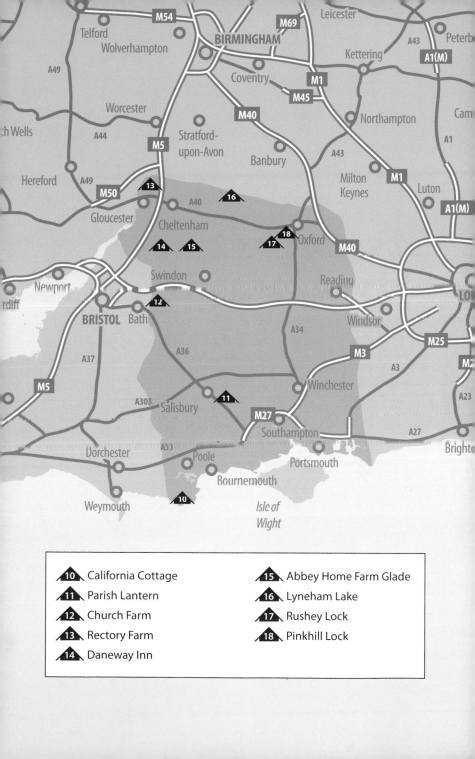

10 California Cottage
11 Parish Lantern
12 Church Farm
13 Rectory Farm
14 Daneway Inn
15 Abbey Home Farm Glade
16 Lyneham Lake
17 Rushey Lock
18 Pinkhill Lock

Priests Way
Swanage
Dorset BH19 2RS
(Don't use postcode
in GPS – see website
for directions.)

Karen Delahay
01929 425049
queries@californiabarn.co.uk
www.californiabarn.co.uk
OS Landranger: 195 (SZ 019 777)

THE BASICS
Size: ⅖ acre.
Pitches: 15 (0 hardstanding).
Terrain: Gently sloping.
Shelter: Trees to south west.
View: Surrounding fields.
Waterside: No.
Electric hook-ups: No.
Noise/Light/Olfactory pollution:
2 mysterious bright lights about a mile
away; some steam-train hoots.

THE FACILITIES
Loos: 2M 2W. **Showers**: No.
Other facilities: Outdoor washing-up area.
Stuff for children: No.
Recycling: Bottles, cans, plastics.

THE RULES
Dogs: If well behaved.
Fires: Designated firepit by loo block;
BBQs off grass. **Other**: Groups can now
book the entire field.

PUB LIFE
Black Swan Inn (free house), High
Street, Swanage (1 mile) – good food
and frequent live folk and blues music;
open Mon–Sat 5.30–11pm, Sun 12–
2.30pm & 5.30–11pm; food served (gluten-
free menu available) Mon–Sat 6–8.45pm,
Sun 12–2pm & 6–8.45pm; 01929 423846;
www.blackswanswanage.co.uk.
Or if you fancy a walk across the fields, try
the **Square and Compass** (free house),
Worth Matravers (4 miles) – pub with its
own fossil museum and jazz festival, and
where the only food served is pies and
pasties (veggie ones available too); open
12–11pm 7D during summer; pasties

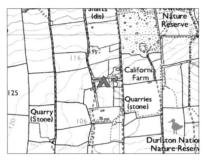

served all day; 01929 439229;
www.squareandcompasspub.co.uk.

SHOP
Costcutter, Herston (1 mile) – mini
supermarket, newspapers, off licence;
7am–8pm 7D; 01929 422549.

THERE AND AWAY
Train station: Wareham (10 miles) –
London to Weymouth line. The hourly
bus no. 40 (www.wdbus.co.uk) runs from
Wareham station to Swanage.

OUT AND ABOUT
Swanage Railway (1¼ miles) – 6 miles of
heritage railway over the beautiful Purbeck
Hills via Corfe Castle; Swanage to Norden
adult return £10.50, child £7, family £30
– discounted tickets available; 01929
425800; www.swanagerailway.co.uk.
Studland Beach and Nature Reserve
(5 miles) – 3 miles of sandy beaches and
a haven for rare birds and wildlife; free;
always open; 01929 450259; NT site.

DORSET

open	Variable: ring for details
tiny campsites' rating	★ ★
friendliness	☺ ☺
cost	BP ££, Couple ££, Family ££££

Among the many charms of California Cottage are the somewhat convoluted directions for getting there. These take you through a munchkinland mobile-home park, over a hill (on a rough track rather than a yellow brick road) and through various gates, until suddenly you've arrived in a small field by a quarry just two fields away from the sea.

The sense of it being your own private plot of land is accentuated by the lack of any adjacent buildings and the thoroughgoing rusticity of the facilities. A washing-up sink stands in the open air next to a standpipe, while a muddy path, charmingly lit at night by a line of solar lights, leads down into a copse that hides the toilet block. The only light in the loos comes from a tiny LED fixture, so do remember to take a torch along. This is not a site for those who, when they say the word 'camping', are actually thinking the word 'glamping'.

Next to the ablutions block is a firepit around which sit plastic chairs, while a pile of crates stands ready to be broken up into fuel for the flames.

Walk out the other side of the copse, and in two minutes you'll find yourself in Durlston Country Park (www.durlston.co.uk), a wonderland of wild flowers, tumbling ravines and ragged cliffs, along which runs the South West Coast Path (www.southwestcoastpath.com). The cliffs are also home to the Tilly Whim Caves, a whale-watching hide and the Seventhwave café/bar.

11 **Parish Lantern**

Romsey Road
Whiteparish
Salisbury
Wiltshire
SP5 2SA

Paul and Lorraine Cooper
01794 884392
paul@theparishlantern.co.uk
www.theparishlantern.co.uk
Landranger: 184 (SU 248 237)

THE BASICS
Size: ⅖ acre.
Pitches: 5 (1 hardstanding).
Terrain: Flat.
Shelter: On all sides except to south-east.
View: Across a field.
Waterside: No.
Electric hook-ups: 2.
Noise/Light/Olfactory pollution: Leave-taking at pub.

THE FACILITIES
Loos: 1M 2W. **Showers**: No.
Other facilities: No.
Stuff for children: No.
Recycling: No.

THE RULES
Dogs: On leads.
Fires: No open fires; BBQs off grass.
Other: No.

PUB LIFE
Parish Lantern (free house) – open
Mon–Thur 11.30am–2.30pm & 5–11pm,
Fri–Sun 11.30am–11pm; food served
12–2pm & 6.30–9pm 7D.

SHOP
Whiteparish PO (¼ mile) – basics plus a
small off licence; open Mon–Wed 7.30am–
5.30pm, Thur–Fri 7.30am–7pm, Sat
8.30am–6pm, Sun till 4pm; 01794 884221.

THERE AND AWAY
Train station: Dean (2½ miles) – Salisbury
to Southampton line. No direct bus service
onward to Whiteparish, so hop into a taxi.

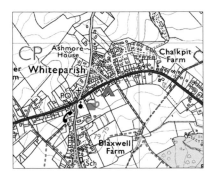

OUT AND ABOUT
The New Forest (½ mile) – covering an
area of about 220 square miles, there's
as much walking, cycling and wildlife-
watching on offer to fulfil the heart's
desire of any man, woman or child;
www.new-forest-national-park.com.
Stonehenge, nr Amesbury (18 miles)
– where the dewdrops cry and the cats
miaow, and huge 5,000-year-old stones
from the Preseli Mountains continue to
puzzle all comers; adult £7.50, child (5–15)
£4.50, family £19.50; open daily June to
August 9am–7pm (opening hours vary
for the rest of the year); 01980 622833;
www.english-heritage.org.uk.
Salisbury (9 miles) – a city with an
inspiring medieval cathedral (01722
555120; www.salisburycathedral.org.uk),
an enticing little museum (01722 332151;
bit.ly/nWJOUr), a great number of fairs
and festivals, and much else besides.

open	All year
tiny campsites' rating	★
friendliness	☺ ☺
cost	BP ££, Couple ££, Family ££

Once upon a time, the flat greensward behind the Parish Lantern pub was a daring fusion that challenged our ideas of what constituted reality. The area was at once beer garden, campsite and adventure playground – a veritable Schrödinger's cat, but with three simultaneous states rather than a paltry two. It is perhaps, then, an act of charity that the owners have decided to stop blowing the minds of drinkers, campers and children by separating the beer garden from the campsite and doing away with the playground altogether. Furthermore, the chickens that strutted and fretted their hour in a long run are heard no more. They have, however, been replaced by other chickens. If that's not a metaphor for something, I don't know what it is.

The view from the campsite, though not spectacular, is one that soothes the soul: an open vista across a field to woods and low hills beyond. Closer to home, the loos are available only during the pub's opening hours, so it's advisable to time your visits wisely.

The village of Whiteparish is just outside the northern edge of the New Forest, Henry VIII's former hunting ground and now the des res of wild ponies as well as five different sorts of deer, three types of snake (adder, smooth and grass), newts, frogs, toads and Britain's rarest reptile, the sand lizard. To maximise your chances of spotting some of the forest's littler inhabitants, hit the one-and-a-half-mile reptile trail that loops out from the New Forest Reptile Centre (bit.ly/uu9VHf).

Monkton Farleigh
Bradford-on-Avon
Wiltshire
BA15 2QJ

Chris and Di Tucker

01225 858583 & 07803 966798

reservations@churchfarmmonktonfarleigh.co.uk

www.churchfarmmonktonfarleigh.co.uk

OS Landranger: 173 (ST 808 651)

THE BASICS
Size: ⅘ acre.
Pitches: 10 (0 hardstanding).
Terrain: Mainly sloping.
Shelter: A long hedge.
View: Westbury White Horse, Salisbury Plain.
Waterside: Pond at bottom of field.
Electric hook-ups: No.
Noise/Light/Olfactory pollution: Occasional neighs and stomping of horses' hooves; RAF airfield nearby (though now closed to all large transport aircraft).

THE FACILITIES
Loos: 1M 1W. **Showers**: 1M 1W (free).
Other facilities: Outdoor heated pool, washing-up area, microwave, kettle.
Stuff for children: Tree swing, slide.
Recycling: Glass.

THE RULES
Dogs: Under control.
Fires: No open fires; BBQs off grass.
Other: Don't feed the horses.

PUB LIFE
King's Arms (Punch Taverns), Monkton Farleigh (¼ mile) – a former manor house now decked out with classy cushioned pews, big sofas, subdued lighting and soothing Röyksopp sounds; open Mon–Sat 12–11pm(ish) – depending on custom, Sun till 7.30pm; food served Mon–Fri 12–3pm & 6–10pm, Sat 12–10pm, Sun till 7.30pm; 01225 858705; www.kingsarms-bath.co.uk.

SHOP
Monkton Farleigh PO (¼ mile) – small but comprehensive shop with a range from

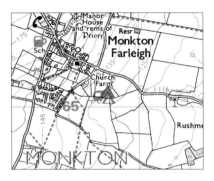

super cheap Euroshopper food to less cheap organics; open Mon–Fri 9am–1pm & 2–5.30pm, Sat 9am–1pm; 01225 858258.

THERE AND AWAY
Train station: Bradford-on-Avon (4¼ miles) – Bath to Trowbridge line. Libra Travel's bus no. 96 travels occasionally from Bradford-on-Avon to Monkton Farleigh.

OUT AND ABOUT
Bath (5 miles) – founded by the Romans as Aquae Sulis and since established as a tourist magnet by John Wood, architect of the city's famous Circus (setting for many a period drama), and Jane Austen, author and astute commentator on social mores; www.visitbath.co.uk.
Bradford-on-Avon (4 miles) – lovely small town, also established by those busy Romans, boasting a Saxon church that was hidden for hundreds of years and oodles of venerable Bath Stone buildings; 01225 865797 (tourist information centre); www.bradfordonavon.co.uk.

open	All year
tiny campsites' rating	★ ★
friendliness	☺ ☺
cost	BP ££, Couple ££, Family ££

The village of Monkton Farleigh, if not necessarily posh, certainly strikes the casual visitor as well-heeled. The pub injects a dose of cosmopolitan cool into this quiet chunk of countryside, the village shop is piled high with organic produce and the cars standing outside the neat stone cottages are shiny and German. Even Church Farm is not a farm in the usual arable/livestock sense, but is populated exclusively by horses who roam its 50 acres looking for trouble – but rarely finding it.

It's a pleasure, then, to discover that there are no airs or graces about the campsite itself. A simple field slopes down a hillside and enjoys a phenomenal vista of the countryside below. In the distance, the Westbury White Horse is caught in perpetual inertia contemplating the Bratton Downs, while to its left rises Caen Hill with Salisbury Plain beyond.

The loos and showers are in a large barn that also stables horses – you pass them on your way in and out – which is unusual for a campsite to say the least. However, even that is trumped by the outdoor heated pool, which is available to campers from lunchtime until 3pm each day in summertime for £3 a pop.

Walkers will relish the jaunt up a hill called Farleigh Rise, which takes off from the north end of the village, while cyclists can drop down to the Kennet and Avon Canal to enjoy a cycle path that stretches from Bath all the way to Reading.

13 Rectory Farm

Lawn Road
Ashleworth
Gloucestershire
GL19 4JL

Mr and Mrs MG Houldey
01452 700664
a.houldey@btinternet.com
www.rectoryfarm-caravanandcamping.com
Landranger: 162 (SO 802 262)

THE BASICS
Size: ⅖ acre.
Pitches: Variable (0 hardstanding).
Terrain: Flat.
Shelter: Yes.
View: Adjoining fields replete with sheep.
Waterside: No.
Electric hook-ups: No.
Noise/Light/Olfactory pollution: Some traffic noise from A417 across the fields.

THE FACILITIES
Loos: 1U. **Showers**: 1U (free).
Other facilities: CDP.
Stuff for children: Trampoline.
Recycling: Everything.

THE RULES
Dogs: On leads (there are sheep about).
Fires: No open fires; BBQs off grass.
Other: No.

PUB LIFE
Watersmeet Country Inn (free house), Hartpury (¼ miles by footpath) – a hotel bar with a log fire, its own 10-acre wood and 3 lakes; open 8.30am–'midnight(ish)'; breakfast served 8.30–9.30am 7D; food served Mon–Fri 12–2.30pm & 6.30–8.45pm, Sat 12–9pm, Sun till 7.30pm; 01452 700358; www.watersmeetcountryinn.co.uk.

SHOP
Ashleworth PO (¾ mile) – basics and off licence; open Mon–Fri 7.30am–1pm & 2–5.30pm, Sat 7.30am–1pm; 01452 700215. **St George's Bakery**, Corse (½ mile) – fresh bread and other delights; open Mon–Fri 8.30am–6pm, Sat 9am–1pm; 01452 700234.

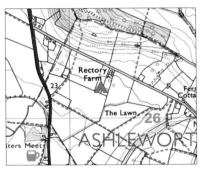

THERE AND AWAY
Train station: Gloucester (7¼ miles) – London to Gloucester line. Regular buses run between Gloucester and Tewkesbury, stopping near the site.

OUT AND ABOUT
Severn Way, Haw Bridge (3¾ miles) – the longest river walk in Britain, a full 210 miles from Plynlimon in Wales to the Bristol Channel; bit.ly/o8tisR.
Gloucester (7 miles) – a compact city packed with delights from the cathedral to the Victorian docks; 01452 396396 (tourist information office); www.gloucester.gov.uk/tourism.
Malvern Hills (8 miles) – a glorious 8-mile ridge that resembles a scale model of a 'proper' mountain range like Snowdonia, the Cairngorms or indeed the Himalayas (George Mallory practised here for his ill-fated assault on Everest); 01684 892002; www.malvernhills.org.uk.

open	Easter to October
tiny campsites' rating	★
friendliness	☺ ☺
cost	BP ££, Couple ££, Family ££

If you head west out of the Cotswolds and stop before you reach the Wye Valley you'll find yourself in an area of Gloucestershire that remains largely uncharted. Here the River Severn slides its way calmly through flat fields in which simple labourers toil away with mattock and scythe until their daily bread is won. Or so it once was, probably. In the midst of what is now a thoroughly modern rural landscape sits Rectory Farm, a modest 60-acre sheep farm located just outside the quiet village of Ashleworth.

The camping area has the feel of a back garden crossed with a farm site. On one side there are flowerbeds spread out around the owners' house, while on the other a flock of sheep mosey about mulling over which juicy blade of grass to go for next. A static caravan is tucked away to one side (it sleeps up to 6 if you fancy renting it), while a trampoline provides children with endless hours of bouncy giggles. Perhaps most excitingly, there is now a loo and shower on site.

If you visit around August Bank Holiday time you'll be able to experience one of the local artistic competitions that take place in Ashleworth (a mile to the east) in the run up to the village's annual show. Past years' creative battles have included making scarecrows and decorating wheelie bins, so expect the unexpected.

Meanwhile, rather more prosaically, the site is just two fields away from a pub (actually a hotel bar, but that does mean it serves food from 8.30am, which is definitely a bonus if you're a few cornflakes short of a breakfast).

Daneway
Sapperton
Cirencester
Gloucestershire
GL7 6LN

Richard and Elizabeth Goodfellow
01285 760297
info@thedaneway.com
www.thedaneway.com
Landranger: 163 (SO 939 033)

THE BASICS
Size: ⅗ acre.
Pitches: 8 (0 hardstanding).
Terrain: Some flat, some slopey, some bumpy.
Shelter: All sides.
View: A little way up the Dane Valley.
Waterside: Disused Thames and Severn Canal.
Electric hook-ups: No.
Noise/Light/Olfactory pollution: No.

THE FACILITIES
Loos: 1U. **Showers**: 1U (free).
Other facilities: No.
Stuff for children: No.
Recycling: Glass, paper, plastics.

THE RULES
Dogs: If well behaved (livestock next door).
Fires: No open fires; BBQs off grass.
Other: No large groups.

PUB LIFE
Daneway Inn (free house) – friendly, rustic pub; open-mic music night Tuesday; open Mon–Fri 11am–2.30pm & 6.30–11pm (shut Mon eves), w/es 11am–11pm; food served 12–2pm & 7–9pm 7D (except Mon eves).

SHOP
Oakridge Lynch PO (2½ miles) – essentials, newspapers, a small off licence and an internet café; open Mon–Fri 8am–7pm, Sat 8am–2pm, Sun till 1pm; 01285 760239.

THERE AND AWAY
Train station: Kemble (6 miles) – London to Gloucester line. The Cotswold Green bus

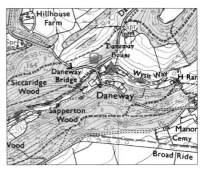

no. 54/54A runs 4 times a day from Stroud train station to Sapperton, a 10-minute walk from the site.

OUT AND ABOUT
Thames Path (4½ miles) – the source of the Thames is but a 90-minute ramble away, making the Daneway a great spot to start or finish a jaunty river trek; 01865 810224; see www.nationaltrail.co.uk.
Cotswold Water Park (9½ miles) – 150 lakes in 40 square miles of parkland, with a huge range of activities to try out on land or water, from paintballing to wakeboarding; 01793 752413; www.waterpark.org. (Also accessible from Abbey Home Farm Glade, p52)

open	March to end September
tiny campsites' rating	★ ★
friendliness	☺ ☺ ☺
cost	BP ££, Couple ££, Family ££

Richard, the landlord of the Daneway Inn, is apt to refer to the experience of spending the night at his campsite as 'camping *sauvage*', and indeed it does take pub camping off to a very unusual place. Rather than a neat and trim level site, the field next to the Daneway careers off around a corner into a wood and slopes down to a long-disused canal which, in heavy rain, is liable to flood. Fortunately, there's plenty of space high enough above the canal (that looks like a mere stream nowadays) for this not to pose too much of a problem. The grass is also left long enough for the place to look refreshingly untamed, and the picture is completed by the many wild plants that grow up through it.

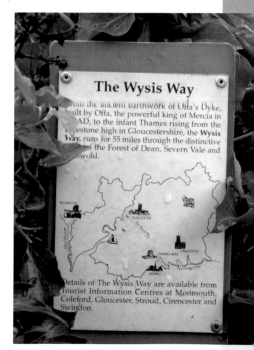

The inn itself is one of those perfect off-the-beaten-track pubs that other people brag about discovering, but which seldom seem to crop up on one's own travels. Originally built as three cottages in 1784 for navvies digging the canal, it serves real ale, has open-mic music nights ('everyone welcome'), and boasts an astonishing floor-to-ceiling carved fireplace rescued from what must have been a huge house.

As for the conveniences, the men used to get the better deal here, with only the gents' being open all hours. Now, however, there's a smart new unisex loo and, heavens, even a shower. Any more of this sort of behaviour and the Daneway's camping *sauvage* experience might become decidedly 'camping *doux*'.

Abbey Home Farm Glade

The Organic Farm Shop
Burford Road
Cirencester
Gloucestershire
GL7 5HF

Will and Hilary Chester-Master
01285 640441
hilary@theorganicfarmshop.co.uk
www.theorganicfarmshop.co.uk
OS Landranger: 163 (SP 042 037)

THE BASICS
Size: 2 little clearings x ¹⁄₄₀ acre.
Pitches: 4 (0 hardstanding). Max. 8 people
per night.
Terrain: Flat.
Shelter: Yes.
View: No.
Waterside: No.
Electric hook-ups: No.
Noise/Light/Olfactory pollution: No.

THE FACILITIES
Loos (compost): 1U. **Showers**: No.
Other facilities: No.
Stuff for children: Woodland to explore;
colourful totem poles to run around.
Recycling: Everything.

THE RULES
Dogs: No. **Fires**: Open fires in tractor wheel
(firewood £5/bag).
Other: 2-night minimum stay; take all
non-recyclable rubbish away with you.

PUB LIFE
The Village Pub (free house), Barnsley
(3½ miles) – yes, the pub is actually called
that; it's very pretty and a swanky gastro
affair to boot (and yes, it's a different
Barnsley); open Mon–Thur 11am–3.30pm
& 6–11pm, Fri–Sat 11am–11pm, Sun
till 10.30pm; food served Mon–Fri
12–2.30pm & 6–9.30pm, Sat 12–3pm
& 6–9.30pm, Sun 12–3pm & 6–9pm;
01285 740421; www.thevillagepub.co.uk.

SHOP
Abbey Home Farm's extensive onsite
Organic Farm Shop is full of delicious
food (much of which is grown just outside

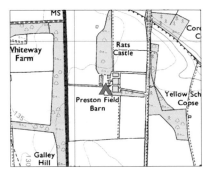

the door), as well as ethnicky clothes and
even handmade furniture – there's also
a funky café; shop open Tue–Thur &
Sat 9am–5pm, Fri 9am–6.30pm, Sun
11am–3pm (closed Mon); café open
Tue–Thur 9am–4.30pm, Fri–Sat till 5pm,
Sun 11am–4pm.

THERE AND AWAY
Train station: Kemble (7 miles) – London
to Gloucester line. Bus no. 855 runs from
Kemble station to Cirencester, stopping at
Stow Lodge, from where it's a 20-minute
walk (www.pulhamscoaches.com).

OUT AND ABOUT
Corinium Museum, Cirencester (2¼ miles)
– one of the nation's largest collections of
Romano–British bits and bobs in what was
the empire's second largest British town;
adult £4.80, child (5–16) £2.40, U5 free,
family discount 10 per cent; open Mon–Sat
10am–5pm, Sun 2–5pm; 01285 655611.
Cotswold Water Park (see Daneway Inn
entry, p50).

open	Easter to Halloween
tiny campsites' rating	★ ★
friendliness	☺ ☺ ☺
cost	BP £££££, Couple £££££, Family £££££

One of the many joys of owning an immense organic farm is that you can put two campsites on it and neither of them need know of the other's existence. So it is at Abbey Home Farm, where Will and Hilary Chester Master's generous slice of Gloucestershire (a thumping two-and-a-half square miles' worth, to be precise) is home to woodland yurts, a 'normal' campsite and, a whole mile away, an amazing hideaway of a site.

The latter space, called the Magical Open Glade, is in the farm's Deer's Choice Wood, with room for about four medium-sized tents or two family-sized ones. Since the wood was only planted in 1991, the trees are still relatively small, giving campers the best of both worlds: sheltered seclusion and sunlight. To keep it secret and magical, the site has to be booked out in its entirety (£40 per night, minimum stay of two nights and a maximum number of eight people).

A tractor wheel serves as a brazier, and bags of coppiced ash firewood are available to buy at the farm shop, although you are encouraged to scavenge your own ('bring your own bow saw'). A discreet compost loo and a water tap complete the fixtures and fittings. From your base you are at liberty to roam the tracks and paths around the farm, taking in the nearby circle of standing stones (a modern creation, but none the poorer for it) or follow the signposted 30-minute farm walk. Just about the only thing you won't want to do, given that the farm shop and café can cater for your every need and then some, is leave.

Churchill Heath
Kingham
Chipping Norton
Oxfordshire
OX7 6UJ

Mr and Mrs DJ Jakeman
01608 658491
Landranger: 163 (SP 269 224)

THE BASICS
Size: ¾ acre.
Pitches: 8 (0 hardstanding).
Terrain: Flat.
Shelter: All round.
View: Down the lake.
Waterside: Yes.
Electric hook-ups: No.
Noise/Light/Olfactory pollution: No.

THE FACILITIES
Loos: 1M 1W. **Showers**: No.
Other facilities: Angling licence £6/day.
Stuff for children: No. **Recycling**: No.

THE RULES
Dogs: On leads. **Fires**: No open fires;
BBQs off grass. **Other**: No.

PUB LIFE
The Kingham Plough (free house; 1½
miles) – a posh pub/restaurant with tip-
top locally sourced or foraged food (just
don't call it nosh, scran or grub); open
12–'closing time' 7D; bar snacks (like
Cotswold rarebit and sourdough soldiers)
served Mon–Fri 12–9pm, Sat 12–9.30pm,
Sun 12–3pm & 6–8pm; restaurant open
Mon–Thur 12–2pm & 7–8.30pm, Fri
12–2pm & 6.30–9.30pm, Sat 12–2.30pm &
6.30–9pm, Sun 12–2.30pm; 01608 658327;
www.thekinghamplough.co.uk.
Or sample the **Chequers Inn** (free house),
Churchill (1¾ miles) – another pub highly
praised for its food (and posh too, though
not quite as posh as the Plough) – booking
strongly advised; open 11am–10.50pm
(teas/coffees served from 8am) 7D; food
served Mon–Sat 12–2pm & 7–9.30pm, Sun
12–3pm & 7–9pm; 01608 659393.

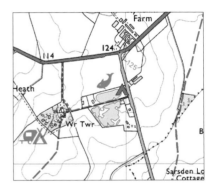

SHOP
Kingham PO (1½ miles) – sells 'almost
everything'; open Mon–Fri 6.30am–7.30pm,
Sat 7am–7pm, Sun (& BH) 8am–5pm;
01608 658235.

THERE AND AWAY
Train station: Kingham (1 mile) – London
to Evesham line.

OUT AND ABOUT
Stow-on-the-Wold (6 miles) – often
crammed to the gunwales with tourists,
but catch it on a quiet day and you
can appreciate why they flock to this
attractive little Cotswolds town;
www.visitcotswolds.co.uk.
Rollright Stones (8 miles) – a monarch
and his court petrified by a witch
(allegedly), the oldest stones having
been put there by our Neolithic forebears
some 5,000 years ago; adult £1, child 50p,
U10 free; open sunrise to sunset; 01608
642299; www.english-heritage.org.uk.

open	Easter to November
tiny campsites' rating	★ ★
friendliness	☺
cost	BP £, Couple £, Family £

What could be simpler? A lake, a few trees, some grass and a loo shed in the corner – all you have to do is supply the accommodation and a will to chill.

The only thing complicated about Lyneham Lake is finding it in the first place. Ordnance Survey maps conspire to confuse in this respect, since they continue to show caravan and tent symbols at a place that's just around the corner (and safely out of sight), which has been a cluster of holiday lodges for some time now. Put the postcode into your GPS and it too will have you heading for the lodges. To find the campsite without resorting to anguished gnashing of teeth, follow the main B4450 from Kingham towards Churchill, but turn off right, down Lyneham Road, and the entrance is on the right.

The area is a cyclists' paradise – there's nothing by way of steep hills, just plenty of quiet roads and oodles of small Cotswolds towns and villages desperate to be ridden to and pootled around in. A day's circular tour, for example, could take in Adlestrop (immortalised in a poem by Edward Thomas), Stow-on-the-Wold, Upper and Lower Slaughter, Fifield and Shipton-under-Wychwood for a pint at the Shaven Crown, a 700-year-old hostelry once used by the monks of Bruern Abbey as a hospice for the poor.

Back at the peaceful campsite, should you eye up any of the lake's fishy inhabitants, just remember you're quite at liberty to photograph any catches you make of the pike, bream, perch, carp or tench, but you'll have to return them to the watery depths afterwards.

Tadpole Bridge
Buckland Marsh
nr Faringdon
Oxfordshire
SN7 8RF

Environment Agency
Lock-keeper: Keith Minns
☎ 01367 870218
🖥 www.visitthames.co.uk
OS Landranger: 164 (SP 322 001)

THE BASICS
Size: ⅓ acre.
Pitches: 5 (0 hardstanding).
Terrain: Flat.
Shelter: Yes.
View: Across neighbouring fields.
Waterside: Yes, the Thames.
Electric hook-ups: No.
Noise/Light/Olfactory pollution: The muffled sloosh of water passing over the weir.

THE FACILITIES
Loos: 1U. **Showers**: 1U (during lock-keeper's duty hours – tokens from lock-keeper).
Other facilities: Outside washing-up sink.
Stuff for children: No.
Recycling: Everything.

THE RULES
Dogs: Under control.
Fires: No open fires; BBQs off grass.
Other: Only walkers, cyclists and paddlers/rowers allowed (no road access). No mooring for boats.

PUB LIFE
The Trout Inn (free house), Tadpole Bridge (1 mile) – a pub that very much styles itself as a dining experience, hence award-winning and on the pricey side; open Mon–Fri 11.30am–3pm & 6–11pm, w/es 11.30am–11pm (shorter hours in winter); food served 12–2pm & 7–9pm 7D; 01367 870382; www.trout-inn.co.uk.

SHOP
Scott's Budgens, Bampton (1½ miles by footpath) – a small supermarket; open

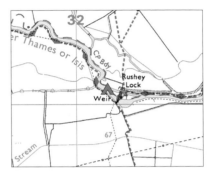

Mon–Sat 8am–9pm, Sun 9am–9pm; 01993 850263.

THERE AND AWAY
Train station: Oxford or Radley (both 15 miles) – Oxford is on many lines, while Radley lies between Oxford and Didcot Parkway. Bus no. 18 (www.rhbuses.com) runs from Oxford to Bampton.

OUT AND ABOUT
Kelmscott Manor, Kelmscott (9½ miles) – a listed Tudor farmhouse that was once home to William Morris of Arts and Crafts Movement fame; adult £9, child (8–16) £4.50; open April to October every Wed & Sat 11am–4.30pm; 01367 252486; www.kelmscottmanor.org.uk.
Buscot Park, Faringdon (8¾ miles) – neoclassical house with some top-notch Pre-Raphaelite paintings; adult £8, child (5–15) £4, U5 free; open April to September Wed–Fri & some w/es 2–6pm; 01367 240786; NT site.
Thames Path (see Pinkhill Lock entry, p58).

open	April to October
tiny campsites' rating	★ ★
friendliness	☺ ☺
cost	BP ££, Couple ££, Family ££

Travel here on foot or by bicycle from the nearest road and you are afforded the pleasure of a mile-long trip along a bank of the River Thames. Canoeists, kayakers and rowers have it even better, since they get to forge along the great river itself, coming eye to eye with ducks, herons, geese and any other birdlife that happens to be swanning around.

Rushey Lock slumbers peacefully in its bucolic setting. There's a fine ivy-covered lock-keeper's house, a few small buildings housing whatever accoutrements are necessary for the execution of the lock-keeper's art and the campsite – a small riverside field dotted with apple trees harbouring fruits of various crunchiness and flavour, and a loo in an unobtrusive building at the far end.

The distance from motorised road traffic lends the lock an atmosphere of unhurried tranquillity. Even the noise from the weir on the far side of the lock blends into a harmonious whole with the chirping of birds and whisper of leaves.

Footpaths extend not only along the river, but north towards the village of Bampton and south-east to Buckland, home of the extraordinary Palladian pile that is Buckland House (privately owned, but you get a cracking view of it from the road) and the 12th-century St Mary's Church, with its Crusader chest (a donation box for the Third Crusade).

Meanwhile, water-control buffs will note that Rushey sports a complete paddle and rymer weir, a system unchanged since its invention in the 13th century.

Eynsham
Witney
Oxfordshire
OX29 4JH

Environment Agency
Lock-keeper: Tim Brown
☎ 01865 881452
💻 www.visitthames.co.uk
OS Landranger: 164 (SP 440 071)

THE BASICS
Size: ⅕ acre.
Pitches: 5 (0 hardstanding).
Terrain: Flat.
Shelter: Under horse chestnut trees.
View: The river and a field beyond.
Waterside: Yes, the Thames.
Electric hook-ups: No.
Noise/Light/Olfactory pollution: The gushing of water through the weir.

THE FACILITIES
Loos: 1U. **Showers**: 1U (free).
Other facilities: No.
Stuff for children: No.
Recycling: No.

THE RULES
Dogs: On leads.
Fires: Open fires; BBQs off grass.
Other: The site is for walkers, cyclists and rowers/paddlers only. Campers must arrive during the lock-keeper's duty hours: April (9am–5pm); May (till 6.30pm); June to August (till 7pm); September (till 6pm).

PUB LIFE
The Talbot Inn (Arkell's), nr Eynsham (2 miles, mainly along Thames footpath) – renovated 18th-century pub with exposed beams, real ales and a seating area outside overlooking a large stream (and, sadly, an oxygen works); open 11am–midnight 7D; food served 7.30–9am (Sat–Sun 8–9.30am), 12–2.30pm & 6–9pm 7D; 01865 881348; www.talbot-oxford.co.uk.

SHOP
Farmoor Stores (1 mile) – general store, bakery, newsagents and (in case you're

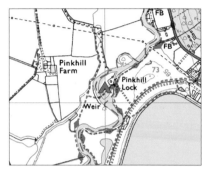

hankering after a bit of biltong) specialists in South African produce; Mon–Fri 7am–6pm, Sat 8am–5pm, Sun 9am–5pm; 01865 862656.

THERE AND AWAY
Train station: Oxford (4½ miles) – London to Birmingham line, among many others. Stagecoach (www.stagecoachbus.com) runs bus no. S1 from Oxford to Farmoor.

OUT AND ABOUT
Thames Path – just cross over the lock bridge to join the 184-mile trail stretching from source to sea; 01865 810224; www.nationaltrail.co.uk/Thamespath.
Farmoor Reservoir, just a field away, is the focus for a number of hides, a countryside walk and a wetland trail; bit.ly/nyFU8d.
Eynsham (pron. En-sham; 2 miles) is one of Britain's oldest settlements, having been around for at least 4,000 years, and home to nine pubs and a biennial open garden festival; www.eynsham.org.

open	April to September
tiny campsites' rating	★ ★ ★
friendliness	☺
cost	BP ££, Couple ££, Family ££

Time was when only wannabe musicians and artists lived on islands in the Thames. Nowadays, in contrast, the river's various isles, aits and eyots are colonised by a rather exclusive coterie who won't admit outsiders, no matter how bohemian their credentials. Happily, there is still a way to get your piece of fluvial island action, and for less than a tenner a night too. The island at Pinkhill Lock is just large enough to accommodate the lock-keeper's house and a small copse, one part of which, delineated by a couple of small signs with a simple tent on them, is the campsite.

Should you amble past the lock-keeper's abode, with its lovingly tended garden (one of the principal qualifications to be a lock-keeper is the possession of green fingers), and through a gap in the hedge, you'll find a wooden shed inside which is a small bathroom containing a clean and modern shower and loo.

But that may be all the walking you'll get around to doing, for this is definitely a site for loafing around on. You can sit on the weir and become mesmerised by the water falling headlong over it, keep watch for the pleasure boats and barges phutting up- and down stream or merely marvel at the patterns the sun paints upon the surface of the river.

If you have a yen to be up and doing, there are several footpaths – including the Thames Path – leading off from the site, and a wildlife-rich wetland area right next door.

South-East England

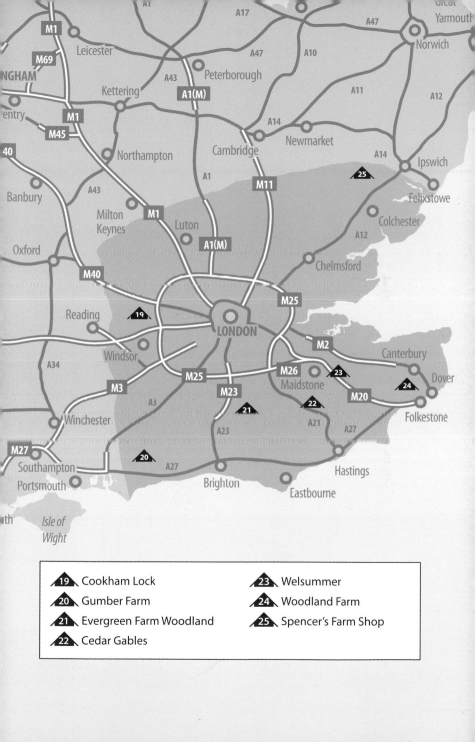

19 Cookham Lock		**23** Welsummer
20 Gumber Farm		**24** Woodland Farm
21 Evergreen Farm Woodland		**25** Spencer's Farm Shop
22 Cedar Gables		

19 Cookham Lock

Odney Lane
Cookham
Maidenhead
Berkshire
SL6 9SR

Environment Agency
Lock-keeper: Adam Benge
☎ 01628 520752
💻 www.visitthames.co.uk
OS Landranger: 175 (SU 905 855)

THE BASICS
Size: 2 x ¼ acre.
Pitches: Approx. 10 (0 hardstanding).
Terrain: Flat.
Shelter: Some pitches.
View: Cliveden Cliffs.
Waterside: Yes, the Thames.
Electric hook-ups: No.
Noise/Light/Olfactory pollution:
Occasional planes to/from Heathrow.

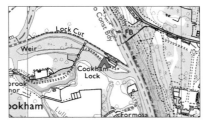

THE FACILITIES
Loos: 1U 1D (radar key).
Showers: 1U (£2.50/2 shower uses, tokens from lock-keeper 'for 8 min./shower').
Other facilities: No. **Stuff for children**: No.
Recycling: No.

THE RULES
Dogs: Yes, under control. **Fires**: No open fires; BBQs off grass (brick pavers available).
Other: Camping only for those arriving by foot, bicycle or self-powered boat.

PUB LIFE
Bel and the Dragon (free house), Cookham (½ mile) – a cosy pub with a gastro menu; open Mon–Fri 11am–11pm, Sat 10.30am–11pm, Sun till 10.30pm; food served Mon–Fri 12–3pm & 6–10pm, Sat 10.30am–3pm & 6–10pm, Sun 10.30am–3.30pm & 6–9.30pm; 01628 521263; www.belandthedragon.co.uk.
Or for a pleasant 2-mile amble west along the Thames Path, there's the **Bounty** (free house) – a legendary maverick drinking hole not accessible by road; open 12–10.30pm(ish) 7D (October to Easter open on w/es only); food served 12–8pm 7D (when open); 01628 520056.

SHOP
Barnside Motors High Street, Cookham (¾ mile) – small news-tob-con; open Mon–Fri 8am–5.30pm; w/es till 3pm; 01628 525555.
Or **Countrystore**, opposite Cookham station (2 miles) – mini supermarket; open Mon–Fri 7am–10pm, w/es till 9pm; 01628 522161.

THERE AND AWAY
Train station: Cookham (2 miles) – Marlow to Maidenhead line. The Arriva (www.arrivabus.co.uk) bus no. 37 runs from Cookham station to Cookham village.

OUT AND ABOUT
Stanley Spencer Gallery, Cookham (½ mile), showcase for the local artist; adult £5, U16 free (with adult); open daily April to October 10.30am–5.30pm; November to March Thur–Sun 11am–4.30pm; 01628 471885; www.stanleyspencer.org.uk.
Cliveden, Taplow (3 miles) – once home to the 'fabulous Astors'; adult £8.60, child £4.30, family £21.55 (grounds only); estate open daily mid February to October 10am–5.30pm, house open April to October Thur & Sun 3–5.30pm; 01628 605069; NT site.

open	April to end September
tiny campsites' rating	★ ★ ★
friendliness	☺ ☺ ☺
cost	BP ££, Couple ££, Family ££

Three cheers for whoever it was at the Environment Agency who thought it would be a good idea to use land at certain Thames locks for camping (see also Rushey Lock, p56, and Pinkhill Lock, p58). This site, at picturesque Cookham, is typical in its unfussy appearance and pleasingly unsophisticated facilities. There are two areas in which to pitch tents: a sheltered one near the lock-keeper's house and a more scenic one on Sashes Island, wedged between the Thames and Hedsor Water. Birdlife abounds: visitors include kingfishers, red kites, parakeets, geese of all kinds and even the occasional hobby.

Toilets are in an eye-catching hexagonal wooden building, and there is a water tap at the back of the shower hut. An onsite refreshments kiosk also stocks bread, milk, tea and coffee (10am–5pm, every weekend from Easter to September – weather dependent – and daily during the school summer break).

To get to the lock, cross the bridge at the bottom of Odney Lane, take the wide path to the weir and then follow the signs. It should be stressed that, as with all Thames lock sites, Cookham is not accessible by car. Furthermore, campers must arrive an hour before the weir gate is locked (April 5.30pm; May 6.30pm; June to August 7pm; September 6pm). You will need to provide a £10 deposit for the key.

Cookham village, though small, boasts one Chinese and three Indian restaurants, a smattering of pubs and the unmissable Stanley Spencer Gallery (see opposite).

Estate Office
Slindon
West Sussex
BN18 0RG

National Trust
Keeper: Katie Archer
01243 814414
katie.archer@nationaltrust.org.uk
bit.ly/elLHu7
Landranger: 197 (SU 962 118)

THE BASICS
Size: ⅓ acre.
Pitches: Max. 35 people (0 hardstanding).
Terrain: Pretty flat.
Shelter: From north.
View: Surrounding fields.
Waterside: No.
Electric hook-ups: No.
Noise/Light/Olfactory pollution: Dawn chorus: swallows, sparrows and wood pigeons in full voice.

THE FACILITIES
Loos: 4M 4W. **Showers:** 3M 3W (free).
Other facilities: Kitchen (inc. oven, kettle and washing-up area), drying room, horse paddock, bike shed.
Stuff for children: No.
Recycling: Everything.

THE RULES
Dogs: No. **Fires:** Firepit and BBQ available (charcoal £5/bag).
Other: No vehicles on site; nearest parking 1½ miles.

PUB LIFE
The George (free house), Eartham (3 miles) is a traditional pub with a beer garden; open Mon–Sat 11.30am–11pm, Sun 12–10.30pm; food served Mon–Sat 12–3pm & 6–9pm, Sun 12–4pm; 01243 814340; www.georgeineartham.co.uk.

SHOP
Elm Tree Stores, Eastergate (4 miles) – a Tardis-like grocery with more or less everything you might need, often at very reasonable prices; Mon–Sat 7.30am–7pm, Sun 8am–7pm; 01243 542117.

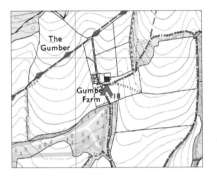

THERE AND AWAY
Train station: Amberley (5 miles) – London to Bognor Regis line. No onward bus route.

OUT AND ABOUT
Slindon village (1½ miles) – a fine example of what many Sussex villages would once have looked like, with some lovely flint and brick cottages; it also claims to be the birthplace of cricket and boasts (ahem) a famous autumn pumpkin display; www.slindon.com.
Arundel Castle (5 miles) – in a very pleasant hilltop location with 40 acres of grounds and gardens, Arundel hosts exquisite works of art, furniture, tapestries, china, sculpture, clocks and good old-fashioned suits of armour; adult £7.50–£16, child £7.50, family £36–£39; open April to October Tue–Sun (& Mons in August) 10am–5pm (last admission 4pm); 01903 882173; www.arundelcastle.org.

open	April to October
tiny campsites' rating	★ ★ ★
friendliness	☺ ☺ ☺
cost	BP ££, Couple ££££, Family £££££

Run by the National Trust and situated on its 3,500-acre ewe-peppered Slindon Estate, Gumber Farm's campsite and bothy are an oasis of remoteness in the crowded south-east of England. The bothy (whose excellent facilities are available to campers) is a converted 19th-century flint barn in a large clearing within an enormous deer-filled wood. The small camping field is right outside it, as is the paddock, in which you may leave your mount should you have ridden in.

The irony is that a farm so lovely – it's surrounded by the sensuous curves of the South Downs and has been eulogised by none other than writer and historian Hilaire Belloc – is habitually used as just a brief stopover by walkers and cyclists attempting either the South Downs Way or the Monarch's Way, both of which run close by (see A Word for Walkers, p186). Were they to linger on the estate a little longer, they could visit Bronze Age burial mounds; a Neolithic flint knapping site; a section of the arrow-straight Stane Street (built by the Romans to link London and Chichester); and a Victorian folly. In World War II, a dummy airfield was laid out here (though only ever bombed once), and air raid shelters and other bits of fakery can still be seen today.

At night, the site becomes a stargazer's paradise, with its huge sky untroubled by earthly lights. Come the morning and the same summer sky is alive with swallows swooping around the plucky sparrows, who make their homes alongside them in the eaves of the bothy.

West Hoathly Road
East Grinstead
West Sussex
RH19 4NE

Jane Warrener
01342 327720 & 07910993622
evergreenfarmcampsite@yahoo.co.uk
Landranger: 187/198 (TQ 388 361)

THE BASICS
Size: ⅓ acre.
Pitches: 12 (0 hardstanding).
Terrain: Mainly flat.
Shelter: Yes, all pitches are in woods.
View: Fields or East Grinstead, depending on pitch.
Waterside: No, but there is a nearby pond.
Electric hook-ups: No.
Noise/Light/Olfactory pollution: A solar-powered light by each pit.

THE FACILITIES
Loos (compost): 1U. **Showers**: No.
Other facilities: 2 brick BBQs; free-range eggs for sale; maps of local walks can be borrowed. **Stuff for children**: Many animals. **Recycling**: Everything.

THE RULES
Dogs: By arrangement (max. 2 on site; £1/ stay). **Fires**: Open fires and BBQs in firepit (bag of wood £5). **Other**: No music (except acoustic instruments); no visitors.

PUB LIFE
The Old Mill (Whiting & Hammond), East Grinstead (¼ mile) – the old mill has, sadly, disappeared, but the stream's still there, as is a working replica of the waterwheel; and you can take breakfast here in the summer too; open 10am–11pm ('often to midnight on Fri & Sat') 7D; food served Mon–Sat 9–11am & 12–9.30pm, Sun 9–11am & 12–9pm; 01342 326341; www.theolddunningsmill.co.uk.

SHOP
Sunnyside PO, East Grinstead (¼ mile) – basic supplies and the occasional surprise;

open Mon–Sat 6.15am–6.30pm, Sun till 12.30pm; 01342 323319.

THERE AND AWAY
Train station: East Grinstead (2¾ miles) – London to East Grinstead line. The Metrobus (www.metrobus.co.uk) no. 84 runs from East Grinstead to Saint Hill, very close to the site.

OUT AND ABOUT
Weir Wood Reservoir (1 mile) – the Sussex Border Path (www.sussexborderpath.co.uk) runs alongside this 280-acre lake, which fair teems with birdlife; www.weirwood.me.uk.
Standen (¼ mile) – a gorgeous Victorian house and showcase for the Arts and Crafts Movement; adult £8.18, child £4.09, family £20.45 (the National Trust calculates entrance fees by throwing a lot of numbers up in the air and seeing how they fall); open mid March to October Wed–Sun 11am–4.30pm (Wed–Mon in August), see website for other open days; 01342 323029; NT site.

open	April to October
tiny campsites' rating	★ ★ ★
friendliness	☺ ☺ ☺
cost	BP £££, Couple £££££, Family £££££

Who would have thought that it was possible to sample the delights of wild camping so close to London? All right, admittedly this is wild camping on private grounds, but it's still not bad for a site slap-bang in the middle of commuterland. Right next to the town immortalised in Alan Ayckbourn's *The Norman Conquests*, the woods at Evergreen seem so far removed from the hurly-burly of the capital that one could almost imagine that it no longer exists.

Excitingly, visitors are whisked off into the 10-acre wood, on a trailer towed by a quad bike, to take their pick from pitches that range from the ultra-secluded to the moderately sociable. There are no standpipes but a large canister of drinking water is supplied, while the loo is a short walk away. Open fires are de rigueur; come in October and you can gather chestnuts and roast them. There's also a discount for anyone arriving by public transport or under their own steam.

The sheep, pigs, goats, chickens, ducks, horses and ponies on Evergreen Farm (which is no longer actually a farm) are pets (yep, even the pigs) and accompanied children can meet up with them for some fussing/petting interaction on request.

Close by there's Deers Leap Park, 240 acres devoted to mountain biking (¼ mile; www.deersleapbikes.co.uk), the Bluebell Railway (Kingscote station; 1¾ miles; www.bluebell-railway.co.uk); and Ashdown Forest (6 miles; www.ashdownforest.org) where Winnie the Pooh once hunted heffalumps.

Hastings Road
Flimwell
Wadhurst
Kent
TN5 7QA

Mrs Morgan
01892 890566 & 07703 024579
info@cedargables.org
www.cedargables.org
Landranger: 188 (TQ 695 335)

THE BASICS
Size: ¾ acre.
Pitches: 30 (0 hardstanding).
Terrain: Gently sloping.
Shelter: Trees all round.
View: No.
Waterside: No.
Electric hook-ups: 11.
Noise/Light/Olfactory pollution: Close to busy A-road.

THE FACILITIES
Loos: 3M 2W. **Showers**: 2M 2W (50p token for 'about 5 min.').
Other facilities: Info shed with settee, books, mobile charger, 2 washing-up sinks, kettle, fridge/freezer, hairdryer.
Stuff for children: Mini adventure playground.
Recycling: Glass, paper.

THE RULES
Dogs: On leads. **Fires**: Use site's own BBQ (£5 bags of charcoal available). **Other**: No.

PUB LIFE
Globe and Rainbow (free house), Kilndown (1¼ miles) – upmarket pub/restaurant serving local produce, with occasional live music and film showings; open 11am–11pm (may close at 8pm on Sun–Mon 'if quiet'); lunch served Mon–Sat 12–2.30pm, Sun 12–3.30pm, dinner served Tue–Thur 7–9pm, Fri–Sat till 9.30pm; 01892 890803; www.globeandrainbow.co.uk.

SHOP
Victoria House PO, Lamberhurst (2¼ miles) – small grocery and off licence, basic fruit & veg, newspapers; open

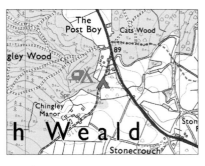

Mon–Thur 6am–7pm, Fri–Sat till 7.30pm, Sun 7am–4pm; 01892 890278.

THERE AND AWAY
Train station: Wadhurst or Frant (both 6 miles) – London to Hastings line. No onward bus service to the site.

OUT AND ABOUT
Bewl Water (¾ mile) – walkers, mountain bikers and horse riders can all tackle the 13-mile track around the reservoir; free; always open; www.bewlwater.co.uk.
Scotney Castle (1¾ miles) – Victorian country house, gardens and 14th-century ruined castle; house and garden tickets – adult £12.60, child £6.30, family £22.50; open March to October Wed–Sun 11am–4pm (for winter opening times see website); 01892 893820; NT site.
Bedgebury Forest (2 miles) – cycle trails, mountain biking, walking, the National Pinetum and Go Ape (www.goape.co.uk) high-wire adventure; free entry to forest (car park charge); open daily 8am–7pm; 01580 879820; see www.forestry.gov.uk.

open	All year
tiny campsites' rating	★ ★
friendliness	☺ ☺ ☺
cost	BP ££, Couple £££, Family £££

If you have a penchant for travelling with the work of an earlier generation of cartographers, you won't find Bewl Water on your map because the picturesque reservoir only came into being in 1975 (when the River Bewl was stopped up). You will have a great time reaching it from Cedar Gables, however; an ancient sunken track spears its way down there, passing fields of wheat and bushes laden with blackcurrants. A left turn at the shore will take you to a bench boasting a view right down the length of the reservoir which, on Wednesday evenings and weekends, is dotted with tiny sail boats, and echoes to the heavy metronomic thud of four-man sculls.

Back at the extremely well-maintained campsite, a gently sloping field sliced in two by a fence provides space for campers on one side and games on the other. Picnic tables grace the well-mown lawn where, at the top end, sweet chestnut trees provide shade from the sun on hot days. It's a shame that the birdsong and the soughing of the breeze in the branches have to compete with the swish of traffic from the A21, but at least the road is hidden from view.

All the loos and showers have been completely revamped, while a small shed houses innumerable leaflets plugging local attractions, a fridge/freezer for campers' use and a few shelves of airport novels to read (or exchange for any airport novels you may have accidentally brought along yourself). There's also a three-piece suite on which to cosy up and devour them.

Welsummer Camping
Chalk House
Lenham Road
Kent
ME17 1NQ

Med and Laura Benaggoune
01622 844048 & 07771 992355
bookapitchatwelsummer@gmail.com
welsummercamping.com
Landranger: 189 (TQ 866 505)

THE BASICS
Size: ⅗ acre & 6 tiny pitches in wood.
Pitches: 20 (0 hardstanding).
Terrain: Flat.
Shelter: Trees on 2 sides.
View: No.
Waterside: No.
Electric hook-ups: No.
Noise/Light/Olfactory pollution: Distant rumble of M20 traffic.

THE FACILITIES
Loos: 3U. **Showers**: 3U (free) including family bathroom with baby bath, changing mat and (ahem) potty.
Other facilities: Shop selling basics, the smallholding's own free-range eggs and organically grown veg, camping supplies; hot drinks and hot snacks served all day.
Stuff for children: Trees to climb, 'places to hide', a large playing field.
Recycling: Everything.

THE RULES
Dogs: Max. 3 on site at any one time.
Fires: Most pitches have a firepit (firewood £3). **Other**: Acoustic instruments and fireside singing positively encouraged, but radios and other electronica frowned upon; no looting the woods for firewood.

PUB LIFE
The Pepperbox Inn (Shepherd Neame), Windmill Hill, nr Ulcombe (¾ mile) – food comes highly recommended (no U14s allowed inside, but there is a beer garden); open Mon–Fri 11am–3.30pm & 6–11pm, Sat 11am–11pm (April to September, otherwise as Mon–Fri), Sun 12–5pm; food served Mon–Sat 12–2.15pm &

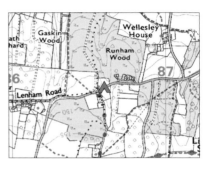

6.45–9.45pm, Sun 12–3pm; 01622 842558; www.thepepperboxinn.co.uk.

SHOP
Lenham Village Store (2¼ miles) – small grocery and off licence; open Mon–Thur 8am–8pm, Fri–Sat till 9pm, Sun 10am–6pm; 01622 858255. Lenham is an attractive little market town whose shops include a deli and a chemist.

THERE AND AWAY
Train station: Lenham or Harrietsham (both 2 miles) – Maidstone to Ashford line. No onward bus service to the site.

OUT AND ABOUT
Leeds Castle (3¾ miles) – sheer stone-fortress perfection; adult £18.50, child £11; open daily 10.30am–5pm; 01622 765400; www.leeds-castle.com.
Biddenden Vineyards (11 miles) – wine tasting and 22 acres of vines to admire; free; open Mon–Sat 10am–5pm, Sun & BH 11am–5pm; 01580 291726; www.biddendenvineyards.com.

open	April to October
tiny campsites' rating	★ ★ ★
friendliness	☺ ☺ ☺
cost	BP £££, Couple ££££, Family £££££

If you're one of those folk who lie awake at night fretting over whether you prefer camping in fields or woods – there's no shame in it, there are millions of us out there – you'll be relieved to learn that Welsummer offers both. (Better still, they now also possess two pre-erected bell tents (sleeping 4+2) and a ridge tent (2+2) for those who lie awake at night fretting that they don't own a tent.)

On arrival, the site appears quite conventional: a short track off a minor road leads up to two small, flat camping fields. However, go through an unobtrusive gate underneath a beech tree and you enter a dense dark wood harbouring half-a-dozen pitches, which can only be described as naturalistic – the owners Med and Laura may have to point them out to you before you realise where they are. This is quite deliberate, as Laura used to camp in these woods as a child and her aim is to offer others a taste of the joys she experienced back then.

Situated on a smallholding with chickens roaming around a copse, bees zipping in and out of hives and a miniature orchard containing native English apples, Welsummer is a laidback campsite that wears its quirky touches lightly (rainbow-coloured windsock, anyone?). Prepare to make friends here, too. This is the sort of place where meals are shared with strangers, especially with those who make the schoolboy error of not lighting their evening fire in time to cook their jacket potatoes by a reasonable hour, so end up stuffing themselves with that haute cuisine of alfresco cooking: the half-incinerated marshmallow.

24 **Woodland Farm**

Walderchain
Barham
Kent
CT4 6NS

👤 Mrs Bennett
☎ 01227 831892
OS Landranger: 189 (TR 207 484)

THE BASICS
Size: ¼ acre & pitches in a wood.
Pitches: 5 in field, 7 in wood
(0 hardstanding).
Terrain: Flat.
Shelter: Yes.
View: No.
Waterside: No.
Electric hook-ups: No.
Noise/Light/Olfactory pollution: No.

THE FACILITIES
Loos: 2U. **Showers**: 1U (free).
Other facilities: No.
Stuff for children: A tree swing, the woods.
Recycling: Paper, glass, cans.

THE RULES
Dogs: If well behaved.
Fires: Yes, in braziers. **Other**: No.

PUB LIFE
The Duke of Cumberland (Punch
Taverns), Barham (1 mile) – a lovely old
pub with a reputation for food and a beer
festival on the first w/e of June; open Mon–
Fri 12–3pm & 5.30–11pm (Fri till midnight),
Sat 12–midnight, Sun 12–10.30pm; food
served 12–2.30pm & 6–8.45pm 7D; 01227
831396; www.dukeofcumberland.co.uk.

SHOP
Barham PO (1 mile) – it's a Portakabin, so
just the basics and newspapers; Mon–Tue
& Thur–Fri 8am–1pm & 2–5.30pm, Wed &
Sat 8am–1pm, Sun 9am–noon.

THERE AND AWAY
Train station: Snowdown (3½ miles) –
Canterbury to Dover line. The Stagecoach

bus no. 89 runs from Snowdown station to
Barham Downs (1¾ miles from the site).

OUT AND ABOUT
Howletts Wild Animal Park, Bekesbourne,
nr Canterbury (8 miles) – set up by the
late John Aspinall to protect endangered
species and return them to their native
environment; adult £19.95, U17 £15.95, U3
free; open April to October 9.30am–6pm,
November to March 10am–5pm; 08448
424647; www.totallywild.net/howletts.
Canterbury Cathedral (10 miles) – the
mothership of the Anglican Church and a
glorious building to boot; adult £9, child
£6, U5 free (free child voucher from website;
or attend a service for free); open summer
9am–5pm, winter till 4.30pm; 01227
762862; www.canterbury-cathedral.org.

open	March to September
tiny campsites' rating	★ ★
friendliness	☺ ☺
cost	BP £, Couple ££, Family ££££

There are some campsites that somehow capture the very essence of camping. The site at Woodland Farm is a simple, sunny, semi-circular clearing in a wood. A dainty apple tree stands in the middle, while a faded green clapperboard hut, containing two super-clean loos and one shower, tucks itself into the trees at one side. With thick woodland all around, the site forms its own little universe.

A dark track leading into the woods promises even greater seclusion. Rough and ready pitches can be found wherever the trees thin sufficiently enough to put up a tent. There's a refreshingly relaxed attitude to the location of pitches too, so you can go anywhere you can find space.

The regulars here often turn the clearing into a venue for all manner of ad hoc games you won't find represented in the Olympics, including a sort of racket-less tennis played with a football and two deckchairs. Should the weather become too hot, or wet, there are some chairs, tables and a bench in a shelter, the architecture of which does its best to defy description: Imagine an over-sized Anderson shelter done in the style of a tropical beach hut. But perhaps the greatest innovation on the site is its braziers. The large metal cylinders once served as washing machine tumblers. The owner's son-in-law mends washing machines, and when they can't be mended, they turn up here.

In the evening, a stroll through the wood and across an adjoining field brings you to Barham, over the far side of which is its greatest treasure, the Duke of Cumberland pub.

Wickham Fruit Farm
Wickham St Paul
Halstead
Essex
CO9 2PX

Paul and Liz Spencer
01787 269476
info@spencersfarmshop.co.uk
www.spencersfarmshop.co.uk
OS Landranger: 155 (TL 833 360)

THE BASICS
Size: ¾ acre.
Pitches: Variable, but max. 5 caravans
(1 hardstanding).
Terrain: Flat.
Shelter: Yes.
View: No.
Waterside: No.
Electric hook-ups: 8.
Noise/Light/Olfactory pollution: No.

THE FACILITIES
Loos: 1U. **Showers**: 1U (£2 per night).
Other facilities: CDP.
Stuff for children: PYO fruit, an old farm
tractor to sit on.
Recycling: Bottles, tins, plastics.

THE RULES
Dogs: If well behaved.
Fires: BBQs allowed off grass; go beyond,
into paddock for open fires.
Other: No.

PUB LIFE
The Victory Inn (independent), Wickham
St Paul (¼ mile) – extremely popular due
to its highly rated food, so do book; open
Tue–Thur 12–11pm, Fri–Sat 12–midnight,
Sun 12–11pm; food served Tue–Thur
12–2.30pm & 6–9.30pm, Fri–Sat
12–2.30pm & 6–10pm, Sun & BH 12–4pm;
01787 269364; www.thevictoryinn.com.

SHOP
Spencer's Farm Shop (on site) – full
of really tasty goodies, local wines and
organic beers, as well as milk and bread;
Mon–Sat 9am–5.30pm, Sun 10am–4pm
(café 10am–4pm 7D).

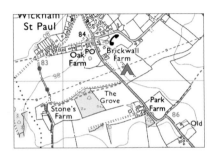

THERE AND AWAY
Train station: Sudbury (4 miles) – Sudbury
to Marks Tey line. One bus an hour (nos.
11, 12 & 13; www.regalbusways.com) runs
from Sudbury to the farm.

OUT AND ABOUT
Hedingham Castle, Castle Hedingham
(4¼ miles) – a quite astonishing Norman
keep with a tremendous banqueting hall,
exquisite grounds and frequent special
events such as jousting tournaments; adult
£6, child (5–16) £4, U5 free, family £20
(try not to swoon at the massive discount);
open mid April to October Mon–Thur
11am–4pm, Sun 10am–5pm, (some
selected dates have restricted opening:
check website); 01787 460261;
www.hedinghamcastle.co.uk.
Dedham (16 miles) – a village on the
River Stour at the epicentre of Constable
country. Georgian houses and craggy
inns abound, while the 15th-century
church and the highly paintable water
meadows on the edge of the village are
also worth a gander.

open	All year (weather dependent)
tiny campsites' rating	★ ★
friendliness	☺ ☺ ☺
cost	BP ££, Couple ££, Family ££

Poor old Essex: forever enshrined in the nation's consciousness as a county of furry dice and *The Only Way Is Essex*. In reality a great deal of the county, especially the area that it ambles across gently undulating fields towards the Suffolk border is chock full of rustic villages whose taste no one would question.

Such is the case of Wickham St Paul, on the outskirts of which you'll find Spencer's Farm Shop, a pick-your-own farm with a café and, as the name imparts, a shop. Its campsite is very much part of the farm: polytunnels harbouring thousands of luscious strawberries run the length of one side, and it's a strong-willed camper indeed who can spend a day here without succumbing to the temptation of grabbing a punnet in the shop and picking-their-own. If there's a danger of you perishing in a strawberry-based feeding-frenzy incident, you can always pop through the hedge and camp beside an orchard instead.

The loo/shower is attached to the shop (with 24-hour access for campers), and is a 200-metre stroll from the campsite, passing all manner of crops awaiting amateur harvest, including rhubarb, plums, apples, boysenberries, tummelberries, tayberries and humble blackberries (though these also grow wild in the hedge and are free). Handily, there are some picnic tables outside the café where you can feast on the banquet of fruit you have picked (though do pay for it first).

It's a shame electricity pylons march through the farm (has any other by-product of modern life disfigured the countryside more?), but they're barely visible from the campsite itself.

East Anglia

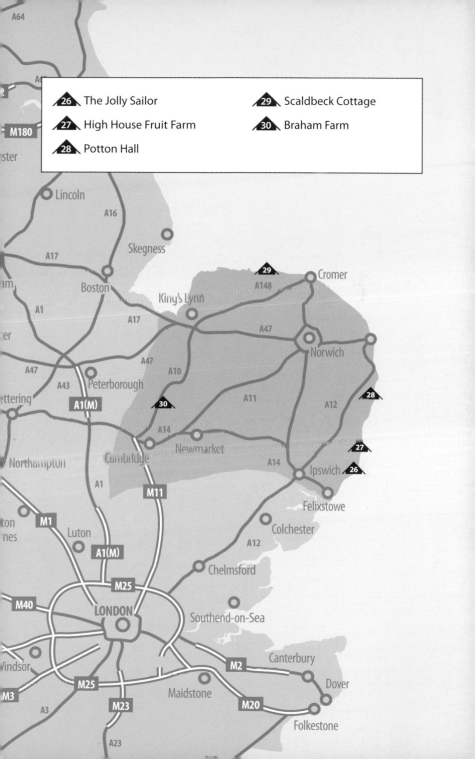

Legend

26	The Jolly Sailor	**29**	Scaldbeck Cottage
27	High House Fruit Farm	**30**	Braham Farm
28	Potton Hall		

Quay Street
Orford
Woodbridge
Suffolk
IP12 2NU

Jane Bloomfield
01394 450243
hello@thejollysailor.net
thejollysailor.net
OS Landranger: 156/169 (TM 423 496)

THE BASICS
Size: ¹⁄₁₀ acre.
Pitches: 6 (0 hardstanding).
Terrain: Slightly sloping.
Shelter: All round.
View: The sea wall and Havergate Island from the beer garden.
Waterside: No, but the River Ore is only 50 metres away.
Electric hook-ups: No.
Noise/Light/Olfactory pollution: Beer garden next door.

THE FACILITIES
Loos: A wetroom with shower & toilet (open 24 hours) & 1M 2W in pub.
Other facilities: Kitchenette including a fridge, washing-up area, 2 electric hobs, kettle, microwave and breakfast bar.
Stuff for children: Swings, trampoline, crab nets, Wendy house.
Recycling: Everything (inc. compost).

THE RULES
Dogs: If well behaved. **Fires**: No open fires; braziers supplied for BBQs. **Other**: No.

PUB LIFE
The Jolly Sailor (Adnams; 10 metres) – mentioned in just about every good food/drink guide on the planet; open Mon–Fri 11am–3pm & 6–11.30pm, w/es 12–midnight; food served 12–3pm & 6–9pm 7D.

SHOP
Orford Supply Stores (¼ mile) – a grocery, deli and café all rolled into one; open Mon–Sat 8.30am–5.30pm, Sun 10am–4pm; 01394 450219.

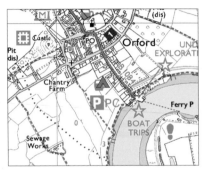

THERE AND AWAY
Train station: Wickham Market and Melton (both around 9 miles) – London to Lowestoft line. Bus onwards – it's a bit complicated (see www.transportdirect.info).

OUT AND ABOUT
Orford Castle (½ mile) – impressive 12th-century 18-sided keep built by Henry II; adult £5.60, child £3.40, family £14.60; open daily April to June & September 10am–5pm, July & August till 6pm, see website for other months; 01394 450472; www.english-heritage.org.uk.
Orford Ness – the experimental weapons facility turned nature reserve; access by ferry only (10am–5pm) from Orford Quay (100 metres); adult entry plus ferry return £7.50, child £3.75; open July to September Tue–Sat and some Saturdays in other months; 01728 648024; NT site. Other river trips available on *Regardless* (07900 230579; www.orfordrivertrips.co.uk) and *Lady Florence* (07831 698298; www.lady-florence.co.uk).

open	All year
tiny campsites' rating	★ ★
friendliness	☺ ☺
cost	BP £££, Couple £££, Family ££££

SUFFOLK

If the Jolly Sailor were the setting for a novel, critics would pounce on it as being too clichéd for words. 'A 16th-century smugglers' Inn with exposed beams taken from wrecked shipping, and inhabited by a ghost?' they would splutter. 'The place where an escaped lady horse thief is dramatically re-arrested?' they would thunder, before shuffling off to mutter at something else.

Except, of course, it's all true: smugglers abounded, the horse thief was a certain 18-year-old Margaret Catchpole who was subsequently packed off to Australia (her 'wanted' poster is in the snug bar) and the ghost made its most recent appearance seven years ago (though there are regular ghost hunting nights held at the pub to check if it's still around). What's more, a sea shanty band plays once a month on a Saturday night. If you want to be transported to a time when they did things very differently indeed, the Jolly Sailor is the place to come.

The campsite is a long, thin apple orchard surrounded by a high hedge. Not only is this a very private and sheltered area, but the trees are so close to each other that, aside from in a mini glade at the far end, there's no room for cathedral-sized tents. However, since there are only six pitches in the orchard, there's loads of space in which to stretch out horizontally.

Orford itself was once a prominent port but now seems content to see out its days as a graceful fishing village.

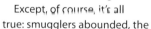

Sudbourne
Woodbridge
Suffolk
IP12 2BL

Piers and Suvi Pool
01394 450263
campsite@high-house.co.uk
www.high-house.co.uk
OS Landranger: 156 (TM 431 527)

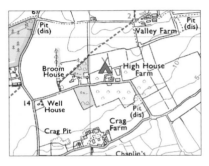

THE BASICS
Size: ½ acre.
Pitches: Max. 15 people (0 hardstanding).
Terrain: Flat.
Shelter: Yes.
View: No.
Waterside: No.
Electric hook-ups: No.
Noise/Light/Olfactory pollution: During the day there's the merry toing and froing of farm vehicles.

THE FACILITIES
Loos: 1M 1W. **Showers**: No.
Other facilities: Washing-up area, kettle.
Stuff for children: No.
Recycling: Everything.

THE RULES
Dogs: No.
Fires: No open fires; self-contained BBQs only.
Other: All stays must be booked in advance.

PUB LIFE
In Orford (2 miles) there are several cracking options including the **King's Head** (Adnams) – a 13th-century pub serving real ales and food made with locally sourced ingredients; open Mon–Fri 12–3pm & 6–11pm, Sat 12–11.30pm, Sun 12–10.30pm; lunch served 12–2.30pm 7D, dinner Mon–Sat 6.30–9pm; 01394 450271; www.thekingsheadorford.co.uk.
There's also the **Jolly Sailor** (see p78) – the new boy on the block (it's only been there since the 16th century).

SHOP
Orford Supply Stores (2 miles; see the Jolly Sailor entry, p78)

THERE AND AWAY
Train station: Wickham Market (8 miles) – London to Lowestoft line. The onward bus journey is somewhat complex (for details see www.transportdirect.info).

OUT AND ABOUT
Orford Castle (2 miles) – (see p78).
Snape Maltings, nr Aldeburgh (4¾ miles) – former barley-malting works that now offers a high-class programme of concert hall events (particularly during the Aldeburgh Festival); boat trips and walks along the River Alde; delectable eateries and a slew of fancy shops; 01728 688303; www.snapemaltings.co.uk.

open	April to October
tiny campsites' rating	★ ★
friendliness	☺ ☺
cost	BP ££, Couple £££, Family £££££

Too often campsites on farms give the impression of having been not just an afterthought, but a thought that has occurred long after the afterthought. If you could hear the farmers' thoughts, they would be thinking, 'Any scrap of land will do, no matter how unsuitable it may be for camping'.

The obverse appears to have taken place at High House Fruit Farm, where the very best spot for camping has been selected: a flat field protected from the Channel winds by attractive trees all round, and yet open to the sun. It's also just a hop and a step from the facilities, housed in a farm building. The trees are, in turn, surrounded by apple orchards, which somehow give the place a summery feel whatever the weather.

The 110-acre farm is primarily one on which cattle graze, but there's still plenty of room for the apple trees as well as for the rhubarb, gooseberries, currants, loganberries, blackberries, cherries and plums, many of which you can harvest yourself (it's a pick-your-own farm too: punnets and measuring scales are available in the farm's tiny shop, where you'll also find bottles of homemade apple juice, preserves and a small selection of veg).

Peace and tranquillity are the order of the day. The farm itself is far from anywhere in particular, and the maximum number of people allowed on the site is a mere 15, so there's always plenty of room to spread out. Please do note, however, that advance booking is mandatory, so don't just rock up here, empty punnet in hand, and hope.

Blythburgh Road
Westleton
Suffolk
IP17 3EF

Jeremy and Helen Hayes
01728 648265
OS Landranger: 156 (TM 453 710)

THE BASICS
Size: ⁶/₇ acre.
Pitches: 10 (0 hardstanding).
Terrain: Flat.
Shelter: On 3 sides.
View: On to the next field with woods beyond.
Waterside: River Dunwich (but you'll have to look for it).
Electric hook-ups: No.
Noise/Light/Olfactory pollution: No.

THE FACILITIES
Loos: No. **Showers**: No.
Other facilities: CDP.
Stuff for children: No. **Recycling**: No.

THE RULES
Dogs: If well behaved. **Fires**: No open fires;
BBQs off grass. **Other**: No children.

PUB LIFE
The Ship at Dunwich (independent; 2¼ miles) – a pub with a reputation for good food, so it's a good idea to book; open Mon–Sat 11am–11pm, Sun 12–10.30pm; food served 12–3pm & 6–9pm 7D; 01728 648219; www.shipatdunwich.co.uk.

SHOP
Lincoln's Village PO, Westleton (1½ miles) – grocery, fruit & veg and off licence; open Mon–Fri 8.30am–1pm & 2–5.30pm (Wed mornings only), Sat 8.30am–1pm & 2–4.30pm; Sun 9am–noon (closed Sun September to March); 01728 648216.

THERE AND AWAY
Train station: Darsham (3¾ miles) – Ipswich to Lowestoft line. Bus no. 196

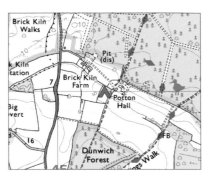

(Minibus and Coach Hire East Anglia; 01449 711117) runs 4 times a day (not Sun or BH) from Darsham to Westleton.

OUT AND ABOUT
Dunwich Museum (2¼ miles) – witness the curious case of the proud city that the sea turned into a small village (with a heath teeming in wildlife); entry by donation; open March w/es 2–4.30pm, April to September 11.30am–4.30pm 7D, October 12–4pm 7D; 01728 648796; www.dunwichmuseum.org.uk.
Southwold and Walberswick (7½ and 4¼ miles) – the former is a very pretty seaside community with its own little pier; while the latter is a beautiful quiet village, made all the quieter by the second homes owned by moderately famous people. Travel between the two across the River Blyth on the Southwold–Walberswick ferry (a rowing boat); 90p per person; June to September 10am–12.30pm & 2–5pm (for non-summer timetable see website); www.explorewalberswick.co.uk/ferry.php.

open	All year
tiny campsites' rating	★ ★
friendliness	☺ ☺
cost	BP ££, Couple ££, Family ££

Potton Hall is real hidey-hole of a site. At a polite distance from the Suffolkian hotspots of Dunwich and Southwold, the site is a good quarter of a mile off the road, up a dirt track. A simple field is sheltered on three sides, while what looks like a sort of mill stream, but is actually the River Dunwich, runs down the length of it, garlanded with bulrushes. The many-gabled Potton Hall, parts of which date back to the 17th century, sits just the other side of a tall hedge. And you might want to keep a lookout for the nightingales, barn owls, red deer, muntjac deer, badgers and voles that often visit the site.

This is a rare adults-only site (see also Silver Birches, p160, and Glenmidge Smithy, p168) and there are no loos or showers, so you'll either have to bring your own facilities or make for the wilds with a trowel and a sense of adventure. However, the owners do run a renowned recording studio on the grounds so you can bring an instrument and a wad of cash and make that album you've always threatened to unleash upon the world.

Dunwich (2¼ miles), which can be reached by footpath through Dunwich Forest, was once the second most important port in England (after London) and possessor of no fewer than 52 churches. The sea has since battered the place – one storm took 400 houses with it – so that nowadays Dunwich barely rustles up enough houses to call itself a village, while the harbour there is sleepy to the point of comatose.

Stiffkey Road
Morston
Holt
Norfolk
NR25 7BJ

Mr E Hamond
01263 740188
ned@hamond.co.uk
www.glavenvalley.co.uk/scaldbeck
Landranger: 133 (TG 004 440)

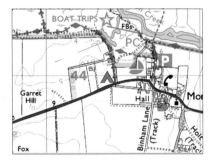

THE BASICS
Size: ⅕ acre.
Pitches: Max. 12 people (0 hardstanding).
Terrain: Very gently sloping.
Shelter: To east and north.
View: The field next door.
Waterside: No, but sea just 150 metres away at high tide.
Electric hook-ups: No.
Noise/Light/Olfactory pollution: During daytime some traffic on main road, 200 metres away.

THE FACILITIES
Loos: 1U. **Showers**: 1U (free).
Other facilities: Outdoor washing-up area, picnic tables.
Stuff for children: No.
Recycling: Everything.

THE RULES
Dogs: Yes, under control (chickens around).
Fires: Open fires allowed in designated area (must bring own wood); BBQ and breeze blocks available.
Other: Don't feed the horses. Not suitable for parties/stag dos.

PUB LIFE
Anchor Inn (free house), Morston (¼ mile) – highly regarded food (book ahead) and friendly new management; open Mon–Sat 9am–11pm, Sun till 10.30pm; food served 12–3pm & 6–9pm 7D (Sun till 8.30pm); 01263 741392.

SHOP
Spar, Blakeney (1½ miles along coastal path) – large convenience store; open 8am–10pm 7D; 01263 740339.

THERE AND AWAY
Train station: Sheringham (11 miles) – Sheringham to Norwich line. The Coasthopper bus (www.coasthopper. co.uk) from Sheringham to King's Lynn stops at the Anchor Inn (see above).

OUT AND ABOUT
Norfolk Coast Path – the 47-mile walk goes right past the campsite and takes in some of the country's most interesting coastline, from salt marshes and mudflats to cliffs (yes, in Norfolk); www.nationaltrail.co.uk/PeddarsWay.
Seal-watching boat trips from Morston Quay (¼ mile) – see the seals (and birds) on Blakeney Point; adult £8, U14 £4; daily sailings (times dependent on tide – see websites); Bean Boats (01263 740505; www.beansboattrips.co.uk) and Temple Boats (01263 740791; www.sealtrips.co.uk). The campsite owners are happy to book one for you.
Sailing School, Morston Quay – various courses for children and adults; 01263 740704; www.norfoletc.co.uk.

open	Easter to October (or later, if weather permits)
tiny campsites' rating	★ ★
friendliness	☺ ☺ ☺
cost	BP ££, Couple £££, Family £££££

NORFOLK

Travel along the main north Norfolk coast road between Sheringham and Hunstanton and, just west of the village of Morston, turn right at a sign marked 'Bluejacket Workshop'. Here be Scaldbeck Cottage, a fine-looking traditional Norfolk flint dwelling with a petite camping field and its own artisan workshop selling handmade furniture, textiles, art and antiques (for a glimpse, see www.bluejacketworkshop.co.uk).

The site is an informal tents-only affair. Access is around the back of the cottage, under trees and past Marans chickens and upturned rowing boats, while a path off through the garden leads to the loo/shower. Do pop a mallet in with your luggage, because although the grass looks soft enough, the ground beneath it is really quite hard after the first inch and will take a certain delight in bending your pegs should you attempt to ram them in with your foot.

Just a five-minute stroll from bustling Morston Quay, the site is ideal for hikers who want a base from which to attempt sections of the Norfolk Coast Path. Simply take the excellent Coasthopper bus to whichever point you want to walk along, then let it bring your weary legs back in the evening.

There's a cooked breakfast available (£7) if booked the night before – either a full English ('a breakfast for kings') with a slew of homemade ingredients or a veggie alternative. In the event of fire, famine, pestilence or the sword, the cottage also has a couple of rooms on a B&B basis.

30 Braham Farm

Little Thetford
Ely
Cambridgeshire
CB6 3HL

Matt Bedford
01353 662386 & 07833 391234
Landranger: 143 (TL 533 775)

THE BASICS
Size: ¼ acre.
Pitches: 4 (0 hardstanding).
Terrain: Flat.
Shelter: All sides except to north (prevailing wind is from south).
View: 2 miles across fields to Ely Cathedral.
Waterside: No.
Electric hook-ups: 4.
Noise/Light/Olfactory pollution: There's surprisingly little noise from the road or the trains, though that's not to say there's none at all.

THE FACILITIES
Loos: 1U. **Showers**: No.
Other facilities: CDP.
Stuff for children: No.
Recycling: Everything.

THE RULES
Dogs: Under control.
Fires: No open fires; BBQs off grass.
Other: In winter only tents and caravans towed by 4WD vehicles are permitted.

PUB LIFE
The Cutter Inn (independent), Ely (2 miles) – this pub/restaurant right on the river has only been open since 2006 but is already a multi-award-winner (and does a gluten-free menu too); open 11am–11pm 7D; food served 12–9pm 7D; 01353 662713; www.thecutterinn.co.uk.

SHOP
Budgens, Witchford Road roundabout, A10/A142, Ely (1½ miles) – a convenience store at a petrol station – not the loveliest of places in the world to visit but useful

in an emergency; open 5am–11pm 7D; 01353 669112.

THERE AND AWAY
Train station: Ely (2 miles) – Cambridge to King's Lynn line. From Ely, the Stagecoach (www.stagecoachbus.com) bus no. 9 passes the farm.

OUT AND ABOUT
Ely Cathedral (2¼ miles) – having seen it from afar, you might as well have a look at what's inside; adult £6.50, U16 free (including guided tour); open daily in summer 7am–6.30pm; 01353 667735; www.elycathedral.org.
Wicken Fen, Wicken (7 miles) – various trails on the National Trust's oldest nature reserve carry visitors over a wetland area brimming with rare species of wildlife (and there's a café too); adult £5.44, child £2.71, family £13.62; open daily all year 10am–5pm (in other months sometimes closed on Mon); 01353 720274; www.wicken.org.uk.

open	All year
tiny campsites' rating	★ ★
friendliness	☺ ☺
cost	BP ££, Couple ££, Family ££

Braham Farm is one of those special campsites that delights far beyond expectation. Look at the map and the signs are not hopeful: there's a railway line to one side and the main Ely to Cambridge road on the other. However, once you've left the frenzied race track of the A10 behind you and have made your way across a field to the farmhouse, a much more promising picture emerges.

Around the side of a wonderful old farmhouse there's a large lawn with a simply fantastic view across wheat fields to Ely Cathedral. At this point you could be forgiven for continuing your search for the campsite in some field beyond, but the joyful truth is that the large lawn is the campsite and the wonderful old farmhouse its perfect backdrop.

But back to the view. Somehow, rather than glimpsing just the very tips of the towers of the elegant house of worship, whole swathes of what travel writer HV Morton once described as 'the only feminine cathedral in England' are visible. If you care to walk to it (it's only a couple of miles away), a footpath from the farm takes you to within a stone's throw (but best not, with all that stained glass about).

Cross another part of this 450-acre arable farm and dive under the railway line, and you can join the 150-mile Ouse Valley Way or the more modest 50-mile Fen Rivers Way (bit.ly/vj7F8d) as they surge along the banks of the River Great Ouse.

Central England

31 The Bubble Car Museum
32 The Green Man
33 Nicholson Farm
34 The Buzzards
35 Forestside Farm
36 Four Oaks
37 The Wild Boar Inn

Clover Farm
Main Road
Langrick
Boston
Lincolnshire
PE22 7AW

Mike and Paula Cooper
01205 280037
mentalmicky2@btinternet.com
www.bubblecarmuseum.co.uk
OS Landranger: 122 (TF 257 503)

THE BASICS
Size: ⁹/₁₀ acre.
Pitches: 5 caravans & variable number of tents (0 hardstanding).
Terrain: Flat.
Shelter: All round.
View: No.
Waterside: No.
Electric hook-ups: 5.
Noise/Light/Olfactory pollution: Traffic on the B1192, occasional tractors.

THE FACILITIES
Loos: 2M 2W 1D. **Showers**: 1M 1W (free).
Other facilities: Indoor washing-up area; small kitchen (charge for use £1/night) including a fridge/freezer and microwave; cheap cycle hire.
Stuff for children: An adjacent flat field is ideal for ball games.
Recycling: Everything.

THE RULES
Dogs: Welcome but best if kept on a lead.
Fires: Firepit; BBQs off grass (bricks available). **Other**: No.

PUB LIFE
The Witham and Blues (Bateman's), Langrick Bridge (1¾ miles) – an American-themed restaurant and bar; opening and food-serving hours long but complex – see website; 01205 280546; www.withamandblues.com. There's also the more traditional **Malcolm Arms** (free house) at Anton's Gowt (4½ miles); open Mon–Thur 11.30am–2.30pm & 6.30pm–midnight, Fri–Sat 11.30am–midnight, Sun noon–midnight; food served Mon–Sat 11.30am–2.30pm & 6.30–9pm (Fri–Sat till

9.30pm), Sun noon–2.30pm & 6.30–9pm; 01205 360369.

SHOP
The site's **farm shop** sells basic foodstuffs, homemade pies and cider, ice cream and free-range eggs. Or there's **Geordies** at Langrick Bridge (1¾ miles); open Mon–Fri 8am–6pm, Sat 8am–1pm; 01205 280311.

THERE AND AWAY
Train station: Boston (7 miles) – Grantham to Skegness line (aka the Poacher Line). Hubbert's Bridge station is closer but very few trains stop there. No onward bus. Cyclists can use the Water Rail Way (see below) from Boston to Langrick.

OUT AND ABOUT
National Bubble Car Museum (on site); adult £3, child £1; open March to November Fri–Sun & BH 10am–5pm.
Water Rail Way (1¾ miles) – a cycle path sliding along 33 flat miles (20 of which are traffic-free) of disused railway line between Lincoln and Boston; bit.ly/nz8urP.

open	All year
tiny campsites' rating	★ ★ ★
friendliness	☺ ☺ ☺
cost	BP £, Couple ££, Family ££

Transported from its former home, the National Bubble Car Museum now lives on a country road between New York and Boston. Happily for fans of tiny motor vehicles, that's the proper New York and Boston, both of which are in Lincolnshire.

Opened in spring 2012, the main campsite consists of a tidy flat field behind the museum. However, the other side of a stand of young oaks, sweet chestnuts and willows lies a small paddock which will, one suspects, become the venue of choice here for most campers. After all, how could one resist pitching in an arena so perfectly formed? Loos, showers and a campers' kitchenette, meanwhile, are also brand new and can be found in the converted barn housing the museum.

As for the museum itself, it originally opened in 2003 to display Mike's personal collection of bubble cars, albeit that the refreshingly dangerous-looking micro three-wheelers also come in many shapes other than bubble. The famous orange Bond Bug is here, as is a monstrous bulbous affair called Bamby (not to be confused with Bambi, though both bring tears to the eyes). There's room too for some scooters and a wonderful wooden caravan from the 1950s that is little more than a Wendy house on wheels. Also competing for your attention are a tea shop (open Friday to Sunday during the day), a farm shop and a side collection of ephemera from the last century, which has every visitor over 40 pointing excitedly and declaring to anyone who will listen that, 'Yes, we had one of those – exactly the same, I tell you.' And it's probably true too, so smile politely but keep them moving.

Church Road
Long Itchington
Warwickshire
CV47 9PW

Mark Carver-Smith

01926 812208

greenmanlongitch@aol.com

www.greenmanlongitchington.co.uk

OS Landranger: 151 (SP 410 651)

THE BASICS
Size: ½ acre.
Pitches: 10 (1 hardstanding).
Terrain: Flat.
Shelter: Yes.
View: No.
Waterside: Yes, River Itchen.
Electric hook-ups: No.
Noise/Light/Olfactory pollution: No.

THE FACILITIES
Loos: 2M 2W (open from 7.30am to pub closing time). **Showers**: No.
Other facilities: CDP, picnic tables; use of the kitchen for washing-up.
Stuff for children: No.
Recycling: No.

THE RULES
Dogs: On leads at all times. **Fires**: No open fires; blocks available for BBQs. **Other**: No.

PUB LIFE
The Green Man (independent) – open Mon–Fri 5pm–midnight, w/es 12–midnight. There's a limited menu 'when we feel like it', mostly of sandwiches and salads, but all five other pubs in the village serve food: the **Buck and Bell** (01926 811177), the **Cuttle Inn** (01926 812314), **the Harvester** (happily, not *a* Harvester; 01926 812698), **Duck on the Pond** (01926 815876) and the **Two Boats Inn** (01926 812640).

SHOP
Co-op Lateshop, Long Itchington (150 metres) – mini supermarket; open Mon–Sat 7am–8pm, Sun 8am–6pm; 01926 812411.

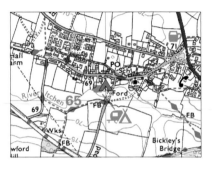

THERE AND AWAY
Train station: Leamington Spa (6½ miles) – London to Birmingham line. Stagecoach bus no. 64 from Leamington Spa stops right outside the pub.

OUT AND ABOUT
Heritage Motor Centre, Gaydon (10 miles) – a collection huge enough to satisfy even the most ardent of petrolheads; adult £11, child (5–16) £8, U5 free, family £34; open daily all year 10am–5pm; 01926 641188; www.heritage-motor-centre.co.uk.
Boating, Leamington Spa (6 miles) – hire a motor boat, rowing skiff, canoe, kayak or pedalo, and take off down the River Leam; from £9/hour; open daily June to August and at w/es other months 10am–5.30pm; 01926 889928; www.leamboatcentre.com.
Leamington Spa Art Gallery & Museum (6½ miles) – LS Lowry, Marc Quinn, Stanley Spencer, Gillian Wearing and more, in the former hydrotherapy pool at the Royal Pump Rooms; free; open Tue/Wed/Fri/Sat 10.30am–5pm, Thur 1.30–8pm, Sun/BH 11am–4pm; 01926 742700; bit.ly/rrO9Su.

open	All year
tiny campsites' rating	★ ★
friendliness	☺ ☺ ☺
cost	BP ££, Couple ££, Family ££

Some pub campsites can be very disappointing: even if the pub itself is lovely, the portion allotted for camping is all too often an unloved crisp-packet-strewn patch of ground. Not so at the Green Man, where, over the last few years, landlord Mark has transformed the tatty green he inherited when he took over the pub. What once was only suitable for holding the annual village bonfire is now a beautiful little patch of countryside. Damsons and an enormous old plum tree circle a picnic table, itself tucked into a little dell beneath which runs a narrow and incredibly lazy stretch of the River Itchen. There's a miniature woodland walk through the trees and each spring a figure of eight course is mown through the high cow parsley. Meanwhile, free-range hens of every hue and shade scratch and strut their way between the tents.

Long Itchington is the self-styled Real Ale Capital of England and it's a claim that is difficult to dispute. It has six pubs, which for a pretty standard-size village is a remarkable feat in itself, and half of them (the Green Man included) feature in the *Good Beer Guide*, while the other three also serve real ale.

There's only an intermittent menu at the Green Man, but a fish-and-chip van stops outside here on Friday nights at 7.30pm and is highly recommended. Also, the five other pubs in the village serve food and are only a short stagger away.

Nicholson Farm

Docklow
Leominster
Herefordshire
HR6 0SL

Tim Brooke
07740 717564
tjwbrooke@aol.com
www.nicholsonfarm.co.uk
Landranger: 149 (SO 584 580)

THE BASICS
Size: 1 acre.
Pitches: 20 (3 hardstanding).
Terrain: Mainly flat.
Shelter: To west.
View: East to Herefordshire farm.
Waterside: No, but there's a lake in the valley below.
Electric hook-ups: 12.
Noise/Light/Olfactory pollution: No.

THE FACILITIES
Loos: 2W 2M. **Showers**: 1W 1M (50p – honesty box).
Other facilities: Microwave, double Belfast sink for washing-up, CDP.
Stuff for children: 3 swings.
Recycling: Glass, foodstuffs.

THE RULES
Dogs: If well behaved.
Fires: Campfires allowed (£6 for a barrowful of seasoned logs); BBQs off grass (BBQ available on site).
Other: No large groups.

PUB LIFE
King's Head (free house), Docklow (2 miles) – run by a chef and her husband (the campsite owner will ferry people here by arrangement); open Mon–Fri 12–3pm & 6pm–'when everyone leaves', Sat–Sun 12–'when everyone leaves'; food served 12–2.30pm & 6–9pm 7D; 01568 760560.

SHOP
Co-op, Bromyard (5¼ miles) – small supermarket; open 7am–10pm 7D; 01885 482975.

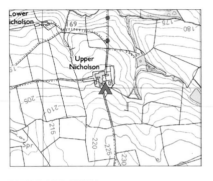

THERE AND AWAY
Train station: Leominster (6 miles) – Shrewsbury to Hereford line. No onward bus to site.

OUT AND ABOUT
Stockton Bury Gardens, Kimbolton (6 miles) – a 4-acre garden with many rare and interesting plants set among medieval buildings including a tithe barn (which is also a restaurant), grotto, cider press and 'a mock ruined chapel'; adult £5 (no children allowed); open April to September Wed–Sun & BH Mon 12–5pm; 01568 613432; www.stocktonbury.co.uk.
Brockhampton Estate, nr Bromyard (7¼ miles) – signposted walks through parkland and woodland rich in wildlife, with wooden sculptures scattered throughout; adult £5.54, child (5–15) £2.77, U5 free, family £13.63; open daily from dawn to dusk; 01885 488099; NT site. There's also a medieval manor on the estate – see website for the complex opening times and prices.

open	Easter to October
tiny campsites' rating	★ ★
friendliness	☺ ☺ ☺
cost	BP £££, Couple £££, Family £££

Goshawks, sparrowhawks, kestrels and all manner of owls have made themselves at home on Nicholson Farm, taking advantage of its lofty position in the north Herefordshire hills. Buzzards, meanwhile, are practically as common as blackbirds, and your chances of staying here and not seeing one are slim indeed.

Even when the air is not filled with predatory birds, the view from this family-orientated campsite is a very pleasant one, taking in the surrounding hills, many of which form part of this 200-acre dairy farm. Owner Tim will give visitors a tour on request; children may even lend a small helping hand if they ask nicely, and will learn that much of the farm's milk winds up as Cadbury's Dairy Milk chocolate.

The campsite, which is located beside the 17th-century farmhouse, is a good quarter of a mile from the main road and down a little dip, so is blissfully shielded from any traffic noise. At the foot of the valley below the site there's a lake heaving with fish of all sizes: fishing permits can be bought from the farm.

Bicycle hire can also be arranged on site. The extremely visitable towns of Leominster, Bromyard and Tenbury Wells are equidistant from the farm and well within two-wheel striking range for even the rustiest of cyclists.

There's also B&B to be had at the farmhouse – including one room with a gargantuan four-poster bed – in case any members of your party are not natural campers. And if you'd like to camp but have no gear, you can now book a ready erected furnished tent (sleeping 5, £40/night including firewood).

Kingsland
Leominster
Herefordshire
HR6 9QE

Elaine Povey
01568 708941
holiday@thebuzzards.co.uk
www.thebuzzards.co.uk
Landranger: 148 (SO 420 629)

THE BASICS
Size: ⁵⁄₁₂ acre.
Pitches: 20 (2 hardstanding).
Terrain: Flat.
Shelter: Yes.
View: Hill.
Waterside: Yes, a small pond.
Electric hook-ups: No.
Noise/Light/Olfactory pollution: No.

THE FACILITIES
Loos: 1U. **Showers**: 1U (free).
Other facilities: Washing-up sink, fridge/freezer, free-range eggs and other organic homegrown produce for sale including meat, tomatoes, salads, plums and apples.
Stuff for children: Animals (with parental supervision).
Recycling: Everything (inc. compost).

THE RULES
Dogs: On leads. **Fires**: Open fires in specified areas; BBQs off grass.
Other: No.

PUB LIFE
The Bateman Arms (free house), Shobdon (2 miles) – 18th-century inn with open fire; open 12–11pm 7D; food served 12–2pm 7D (Sun till 2.30pm) & 7–9pm Tue–Sat; 01568 708374; www.batemanarms.com. For a cup that cheers but does not inebriate, try the **Garden Tea Room and Deli** at Kingsland (2½ miles); open Wed–Sat 11am–6pm, Sun 11am–5.30pm, BH 10.30am–5.30pm; 01568 709142.

SHOP
The award-winning community-run **Yarpole Shop & PO** (in St Leonard's

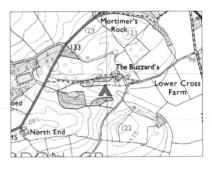

church; 3 miles) – a range of supplies (many locally sourced inc. wines, beers and ciders) and a fab café in the nave; Mon–Fri 9am–1pm & 3–5pm, Sat 9am–1pm; Sun 10am–noon; 01568 780148; www. yarpoleshop.co.uk. Wigmore (3½ miles) also has a community run store; 01568 770307 for opening times.

THERE AND AWAY
Train station: Leominster (7 miles) – Shrewsbury to Hereford line. Elaine can collect/drop off at Leominster station by prior arrangement.

OUT AND ABOUT
Berrington Hall, nr Leominster (8 miles) – neoclassical mansion in landscaped grounds; adult £7.20, child £3.60, family £18; house open early March to early November 11am–5pm 7D (see website for other months); 01568 615721; NT site.
Black and White Trail, Kingsland (2½ miles) is the closest port of call for this 40-mile loop around Herefordshire's black and white timber-framed houses; bit.ly/bAQTLp.

open	All year
tiny campsites' rating	★★★
friendliness	☺ ☺ ☺
cost	BP £££, Couple £££, Family £££

Once you've arrived at the Buzzards, the difficulty is deciding where to go first. The badger hide, perhaps? Or the bluebell-carpeted wood for some bat watching? Or maybe a visit to scratch the ears of Barbara, the big Tamworth sow?

It's hard to believe that this biodynamic smallholding only covers 16 acres, so packed is it with happy diversions. The delights continue at the secluded campsite, which enjoys a private view up the wooded valley. There's a separate, even smaller field for campervans and caravans, while the loo/shower is attached to the main house, a short step away.

Should you care to wander, this part of Herefordshire is packed with things to see and do, including Croft Castle (3 miles; NT site), the 30-mile Mortimer Trail (Aymestry, 1¼ miles; bit.ly/rALE4u) and the Dunkerton's cider orchards and chocolaterie (6¼ miles; dunkertons.co.uk), while each village in the area has its own short circular walks (leaflets available on site).

A good many people, however, simply prefer to take root in the camping field, enjoying the visits from the three friendly cats; soaking in the music of rustling leaves and whispering grass; ambling along to the mere by the woods to commune with the grebes, coots and moorhens; or merely chatting with Elaine, owner of the Buzzards and the very soul of kindness.

Nowadays there's an even more secluded space for those who seriously want to get away from it all: a separate pitch in the small ancient quarry from which the stone came to build the farmhouse.

35 Forestside Farm

Marchington Cliff
Uttoxeter
Staffordshire
ST14 8NA

Chris and Janette Prince

01283 820353

stay@forestsidefarm.co.uk

www.forestsidefarm.co.uk

Landranger: 128 (SK 132 291)

THE BASICS
Size: 1 acre.
Pitches: 17 – max. 30 people
(5 hardstanding).
Terrain: Gently sloping.
Shelter: Trees to south.
View: North towards Peak District.
Waterside: No.
Electric hook-ups: 8.
Noise/Light/Olfactory pollution: The
occasional nocturnal roar of a cow validating
its existence in the field next door.

THE FACILITIES
Loos: 2M 2W. **Showers**: 2M 2W (free).
Other facilities: Washing-up area, fridge,
kettle, microwave, tourist information,
coarse fishing passes, CDP.
Stuff for children: Kids can watch the
cows being milked if under supervision.
Recycling: Everything.

THE RULES
Dogs: On leads at all times. **Fires**: No open
fires; BBQs off grass. **Other**: No.

PUB LIFE
The Dog & Partridge (free house),
Marchington (1 mile) – a Georgian
country inn; open Thur–Tue 12–'whenever
everyone's gone home', Wed from 6pm;
food served Tue–Sat 12–2pm, Sun 12–
4pm, Tue–Sat 6–9.30pm; 01283 820394;
dogandpartridge.homestead.com.
Marchington is also home to **The
Blacksmith's Arms** (01889 569343)
and **The Bulls Head** (01283 820358).
The Barn (1 mile), is an Indian restaurant
on the road towards Draycott in the Clay;
01283 820367.

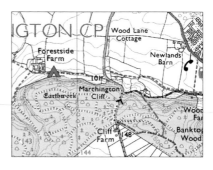

SHOP
Marchington Village Shop (1 mile) –
basics and newspapers; Mon–Wed 8am–
6pm, Thur–Fri till 7pm, Sat till noon, Sun
9am–noon; 01283 821248.

THERE AND AWAY
Train station: Uttoxeter (5¼ miles) –
Derby to Crewe line. Bus no. 402 runs from
Uttoxeter train station to Marchington Cliff.

OUT AND ABOUT
Sudbury Hall & Museum of Childhood,
Sudbury (4¾ miles) – a grand 17th-century
mansion, a childhood museum and host of
special events; joint entry to mansion and
museum: adult £13.18, child £7.09, family
£33.45 (plus discount if arriving by bicycle
or public transport); open on varying days
according to season from mid February to
mid December; 01283 585305; NT site.
Tutbury Castle (6¼ miles) – a prison for
Mary Queen of Scots; adult £2.50, child
(5–12) £2, U5 free, family £14; open April to
September Wed–Sun 11am–5pm, rest of
year w/es only; www.tutburycastle.com.

open	All year
tiny campsites' rating	★ ★
friendliness	☺ ☺ ☺
cost	BP ££, Couple £££, Family ££££

There are some campsites that merely aspire to views and others that have them in spades. Look north from Forestside, a 156-acre organic dairy farm, and you'll enjoy a 180-degree vista that takes in both the Weaver Hills and the Peak District's Dove Valley, and still has room for more around the edges. At night, all those distant parts that looked uninhabited suddenly switch on their lights, presumably for the benefit of those watching from the farm.

The site consists of an upper mown field with a slightly rougher field below for those who prefer their camping a little less refined. As the name suggests, the farm is right next to a wood (listen out for tawny owls in the evening) that rises steeply behind it up Marchington Cliff, giving some shelter to the south. A sort of upmarket timber stable block houses the facilities, which include four highly civilised shower rooms. In the tourist info room there are some laminated maps of a short, circular farm walk to sharpen your appetite for dinner or get the blood circulating in the morning.

At this campsite, your most difficult decision is where you spend the rest of your day, as there are numerous attractions within striking distance to tempt you off the premises (see also facing page), including horse racing at Uttoxeter (4¾ miles) to the heart-stoppingly beautiful Manifold Valley cycle trail (18 miles; bit.ly/tR2Wm5). Don't mention it to the kids, but you're also just a dozen miles from Alton Towers.

Lower House Farm
Whixall
Shropshire
SY13 2NG

Mr Williams
01948 880241
OS Landranger: 126 (SJ 522 348)

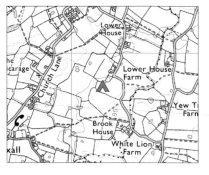

THE BASICS
Size: ⅔ acre.
Pitches: Variable (0 hardstanding).
Terrain: Flat.
Shelter: All round.
View: Into next field.
Waterside: Yes, a large pond.
Electric hook-ups: No.
Noise/Light/Olfactory pollution: No.

THE FACILITIES
Loos (open air): 1U. **Showers**: No.
Other facilities: No.
Stuff for children: No. **Recycling**: No.

THE RULES
Dogs: Yes. **Fires**: Open fires; BBQs off grass.
Other: No.

PUB LIFE
Horseshoes Inn (Admiral), Tilstock
(2¾ miles) – friendly country pub with
three menus (curry, pizza and pub grub)
at very reasonable prices; open Mon–Thur
4.30–11pm, Fri 4–11.30pm, Sat 2–11.30pm,
Sun 1–10.30pm; food served from opening
until half an hour before closing;
01948 880704.

SHOP
Coton Oaks, Coton (3 miles) – a farm shop
and café with Internet facilities; stocks a
few basics, some deli goodies, plus wine
and local beers; open Mon–Fri 8am–5pm,
Sat till 4pm; 01948 840592.

THERE AND AWAY
Train station: Prees (3 miles) – a request
stop on the Shrewsbury to Crewe line.
No direct bus service to the site.

OUT AND ABOUT
Hawkstone Follies (6½ miles) – a
200-year-old fantasia of weird and
wonderful monuments in a land of
caves, crags and woods; adult £7, child
£4.50, family £22; open daily from June
to August, 10am–5pm (last admission
3.30pm; for non-summer opening see
website); 01948 841700; bit.ly/n1TRng.
Whixall Moss (2 miles) – a nature reserve
so large it's visible from space (guided
walks also available); 01948 880362.
The market towns of **Wem** (4¼ miles) and
Whitchurch (5 miles) are also worth a
mosey around.

open	All year
tiny campsites' rating	★ ★
friendliness	☺ ☺
cost	BP £, Couple ££, Family ££

If any site exemplified the concept of 'hideaway' it's this one. First you must find Lower House Farm, which is tucked away within a maze of tiny roads. Then, rather than calling in at the farmhouse, you should proceed to the new dwelling immediately to its left. From here you will be directed on an almost circular tour of yet more minor roads for the best part of a mile, arriving eventually at an unmarked gate in a hedge. Pass through this, across a field and through another gate and you're there. Congratulations. Plans are afoot to construct a track across the fields to link the site to the new house at Lower House Farm, but until then the getting there only increases the anticipation and is all part of the holiday fun.

The rewards for those who make it are superb. About a third of the field is given over to a large pond encircled by trees, topped with lily pads and bristling with water-loving plants. The pond is vaguely Pac-Man shaped (by chance rather than design, apparently), so if you pop your tent into the bit where the mouth would be, you're in just about the snuggest camping pitch in the country: perfect for dropping anchor and lazily observing whatever passing wildlife might choose to visit the pond.

Despite its remote location, there is not only a water tap here but a loo too. The latter is surrounded by a low wooden slatted fence, which is open to the elements but, hey, it flushes (though do remember to take your own loo paper).

37 The Wild Boar Inn

Wincle
Macclesfield
Cheshire
SK11 0QL

- Val Bailey and Alan Critchlow
- 01260 227219
- www.thewildboar.co.uk
- OS Landranger: 118 (SJ 959 671)

THE BASICS
Size: ²/₅ acre.
Pitches: 26 (5 hardstanding).
Terrain: Flat/gently sloping.
Shelter: Room for a couple of tents to hide behind trees.
View: Peak District and Cheshire hills.
Waterside: No.
Electric hook-ups: 4.
Noise/Light/Olfactory pollution:
Occasional traffic.

THE FACILITIES
Loos: 2M 3W. **Showers**: 1U 1M (£1 for '5 min.'). **Other facilities**: Outdoor washing-up area, picnic tables, CDP.
Stuff for children: No.
Recycling: No.

THE RULES
Dogs: On leads at all times.
Fires: No open fires; BBQs off grass.
Other: The site is 'adult-orientated' – if you do bring kids please keep them in line.

PUB LIFE
The Wild Boar Inn (Robinson's; 20 metres) – open Mon–Fri from 4.30pm, Sat from noon & Sun from 11am till 'late' every day; food served Fri 5–8.30pm, Sat 12–8.30pm, Sun till 8pm; 01260 227219.
For food Tue–Thur, try the **Crag** at Dane in Wildboarclough (pron. 'Wilbercluff'); open Tue–Sat 11am–2.30pm & 7–11pm, Sun 11am–6pm; food served Tue–Sat 12–2pm & 7–9pm, Sun 12–2.30pm; 01260 227239.

SHOP
Sutton PO, nr Macclesfield (3 miles) – convenience store and off licence; open

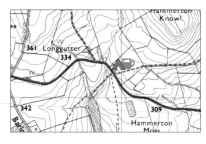

Mon–Fri 6am–7pm, Sat till 6pm, Sun till 1pm; 01260 252438. Outside these hours, there are plenty of shops in Macclesfield.

THERE AND AWAY
Train station: Macclesfield (5½ miles) – Manchester to Stoke-on-Trent line. No onward bus service to the site.

OUT AND ABOUT
Capesthorne Hall, Siddington (11¼ miles) – a Jacobean-style house filled with artworks, plus a Georgian chapel, gardens and lakes in 100 acres of parkland; see website for excitingly complex ticket pricing system (including discounts for cyclists); open April to October Sun–Mon & BH 1.30–4pm (last admission 3.30pm); 01625 861221; www.capesthorne.com.
Lyme Park, Disley (15 miles) – a former Tudor house transformed into an Italianate palace from whose lake a certain Mr Darcy/Colin Firth emerged wet and ruffled around the edges to send a million hearts aflutter; house and garden entry: adult £8.50, child £4.15, family £20.80; open March to October Fri–Tue 11am–5pm; 01663 762023; NT site.

open	All year
tiny campsites' rating	★ ★
friendliness	☺ ☺
cost	BP ££, Couple £££, Family £££££

The Wild Boar Inn is many people's idea of camping heaven. Not only are there astonishing views to wake up to in the morning, at night you can step out of the pub and straight into your sleeping bag. It's a proper pub too, with copper bed-warming pans on the walls and a feeling that if you're inside when it starts snowing you could be holed up for the winter (In reality, this is a somewhat rare event).

High up on a pass between Congleton and Buxton, and remote enough not to enjoy mains water (the pub has its own bore hole), the Wild Boar is a magnet for hikers keen to walk the Dane Valley or the Staffordshire Moorlands, and for less-energetic types who simply want to spend a day or two breathing in fresh hilltop air and gazing into the distance. The pub's very reasonably priced all-day breakfasts are popular with campers and caravanners alike, who can also enjoy live music every Saturday night throughout the summer months.

Unlike the majority of pubs, the Wild Boar has its very own clay pigeon shooting team that meets every other Sunday morning around nine o'clock. If you're a clay pigeon shooter yourself, or just fancy shouting 'pull' before blasting away at thin air, ring Mr Roberts, the club secretary, in advance and he'll do his best to fit you in (01625 614603).

Sadly, nearby Macclesfield station's perversely brilliant platform 0 no longer exists, but there is still one not so far away at Stockport.

Northern England

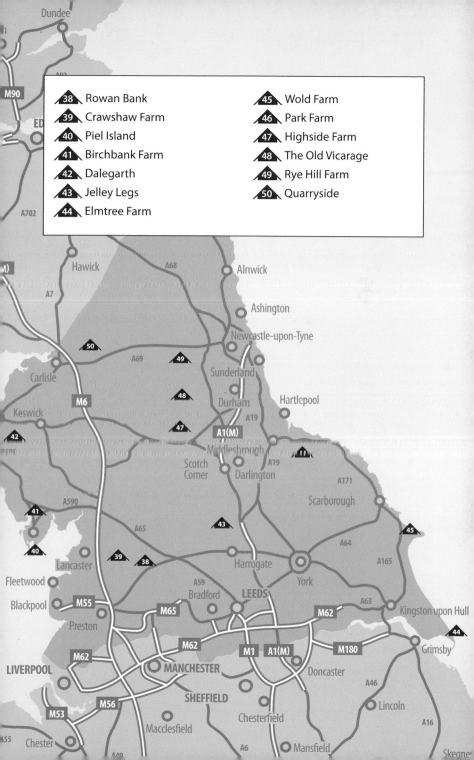

Horton in Craven
Skipton
Yorkshire
BD23 3JP
(Don't use postcode in
GPS – see opposite.)

Mr AC Bancroft

01200 445291 & 07866 050845

Landranger: 103 (SD 873 503)

THE BASICS
Size: ½ acre.
Pitches: Variable (1 hardstanding).
Terrain: Mainly flat.
Shelter: No.
View: A spectacular range of hills and a
small town.
Waterside: No.
Electric hook-ups: 6.
Noise/Light/Olfactory pollution: Some
traffic on the A59.

THE FACILITIES
Loos: No. **Showers**: No.
Other facilities: CDP.
Stuff for children: No.
Recycling: Everything.

THE RULES
Dogs: Welcome – there's a playing field for
them and dog-waste bins are provided.
Fires: No open fires; BBQs well off grass.
Other: No.

PUB LIFE
Cross Keys (free house), East Marton
(2½ miles) – a snug cottage-like pub near
the Leeds and Liverpool Canal; open
12–11pm 7D; food served Mon–Fri
12–2.30pm & 5–8pm, Sat 12–2.30pm &
5–9pm, Sun 12–7pm; 01282 844326.

SHOP
The Pantry at West Marton (1½ miles) –
usual supplies plus a deli, sarnies, hot pies
and coffee to take away; open Mon–Fri
7am–6.30pm, Sat 8am–1pm, Sun 9am–
noon (these hours 'likely to extend');
01282 787640. Otherwise, the **77 Garage**
in Gisburn (3 miles) sells basics; open

Mon–Sat 6.30am–8pm, Sun 7am–8pm;
01200 415953.

THERE AND AWAY
Train station: Gargrave (6 miles) – Leeds
to Settle line. From Gargrave pick up the
Pennine Motors (www.pennine-bus.co.uk)
bus no. 580 to Skipton and from there the
Lancashire United (www.lancashirebus.
co.uk) X80 Ribble Valley Express to the site.

OUT AND ABOUT
Skipton Castle, Skipton (7 miles) –
over 900 years old and still going strong,
despite a history of sieges; adult £6.70,
child (5–17) £4.10, U5 free, family
£21.50; open March to September daily
10am–6pm (Sun 12–6pm), October to
February daily 10am–4pm (Sun 12–4pm);
01756 792442; www.skiptoncastle.co.uk.
Narrowboat trip, Skipton (7 miles) – a
30-minute trip aboard *Leo* or *Sam* on the
Springs branch of the Leeds and Liverpool
Canal: £3 per seat; daily trips March to
October from 10.30am (less frequently
at other times of year); 01756 795478;
www.penninecruisers.com. Also day
boats for hire.

open	All year
tiny campsites' rating	★
friendliness	☺ ☺ ☺
cost	BP ££, Couple ££, Family ££

As a campsite situated very much on the way to and from other places – it's just off the A59, eight miles from Clitheroe and seven miles from Skipton – it would be tempting to think of Rowan Bank as just a convenient stopover. That is, until you see the view. Off to the right stands the vast bulk of Pendle Hill, the first of a huge sweep of fells. The small town of Barnoldswick (if you ever need to pronounce it, go for 'Barlick') tucked under Weets Hill, completes a very agreeable picture.

The site itself is a simple one – an oblong field bordered by a low fence on a 40-acre sheep farm. There are some barns at the far end and a view practically everywhere else. Off site, Skipton offers a particularly good day out if you combine a visit to the castle with a boat ride on the canal; while walkers have a choice of tackling any of the hills they can see from their tents as well as the Easington Fell, to the north of Clitheroe.

The only drawback is that there's no loo here, so unless you bring your own you'll have to use public facilities when you're out and about or conveniences in any pubs and cafés you might frequent. Please also note that unless you fancy being sent to a farm several miles away at the top end of Horton in Craven, don't put Rowan Bank's postcode into your GPS. Stay on the A59 and, as long as you don't miss their signpost, you can't go wrong.

Back Lane
Newton-in-Bowland
Lancashire
BB7 3EE
(Don't use postcode in
GPS – see opposite.)

Martyn and Jayne Bristol
01200 446638
jayne.bristol@virgin.net
OS Landranger: 103 (SD 693 514)

THE BASICS
Size: ½ acre.
Pitches: 9 (0 hardstanding).
Terrain: Gently sloping.
Shelter: Low wall all round and trees to the east.
View: Beautiful hills everywhere you look.
Waterside: No.
Electric hook-ups: No.
Noise/Light/Olfactory pollution: The rooks sometimes like a good squawk.

THE FACILITIES
Loos: 1U. **Showers**: No.
Other facilities: CDP.
Stuff for children: No.
Recycling: Bottles, cans.

THE RULES
Dogs: On leads.
Fires: No open fires; BBQs off grass.
Other: No.

PUB LIFE
Parkers Arms (free house), Newton (1¼ miles) – formerly the coach house of nearby Newton Hall, now a restaurant sort of pub; open Tue–Fri 12–3pm & 6pm–'late', w/es 12–'late'; food served Tue–Fri 12–2.30pm & 6–8.30pm, w/es 12–9pm; 01200 446236; www.parkersarms.co.uk.
Hark to Bounty (free house), Slaidburn (3 miles by road, 1½ miles by footpath) – stone-built pub with lovely beer garden; open 8am–midnight 7D; food served Mon–Thur 12–2pm & 6–8pm, Fri–Sat 12–2pm & 6–9pm, Sun 12–8pm (breakfasts also served daily from 8–11.30am); 01200 446246; www.harktobounty.co.uk.

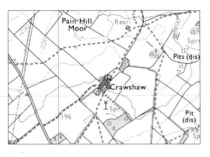

SHOP
Slaidburn Central Store (3 miles) – basics and a selection of pies; open Mon–Fri 7.45am–5.30pm, Sat 8.30am–5pm, Sun 9am–1pm; 01200 446268.

THERE AND AWAY
Train station: Clitheroe (7 miles) – Manchester to Clitheroe line. From Clitheroe take the Tyrer's Tours bus no. B10 to Newton, a 20-minute walk from the farm.

OUT AND ABOUT
Bowland – Crawshaw Farm is in the heart of this area of outstanding natural beauty, which covers 312 square miles of rural Lancashire and north Yorkshire: the vast gathering of fells, rivers, tiny villages and wildlife is a paradise for walkers and cyclists (see website for route suggestions); 01200 448000; www.forestofbowland.com.
Clitheroe Castle Museum (7 miles) – newly refurbished 12th-century keep with interactive museum; adult £3.65, accompanied children free; open daily April to October 11am–5pm, November to March 12–4pm; 01200 424568; bit.ly/mQW4tZ.

open	Easter to October
tiny campsites' rating	★ ★
friendliness	☺ ☺
cost	BP ££, Couple ££, Family ££

Crawshaw Farm is the sort of campsite Britons hold in their collective memory: a simple open field bounded by a drystone wall, with a loo in a lean-to by the farmhouse, and drinking water sourced from a tap coming out of a wall. A footpath goes right through the site, leading walkers off towards Slaidburn, one way and Newton, the other.

Kestrels command the skies above this 80-acre dairy farm, while tawny owls provide an aural backdrop at night. As for the view: bring along some extra superlatives because you'll be needing them. Even though Crawshaw Farm is 200 metres above sea level, whichever direction you look in you're greeted with stonking Lancastrian hills rising far above it.

Just a few miles away, or half an hour's walk via footpaths and a minor road, lies the small village of Slaidburn. A film-location spotter's dream, its stone houses and shuttered windows could easily stand in as a medieval French hamlet, so don't be too surprised if you bump into Audrey Tautou walking down the main street wearing a wimple.

Trivia-baggers will be excited to learn that the nearby village of Dunsop Bridge boasts a telephone box situated supposedly at the dead centre of Great Britain. Installed in 1992 as British Telecom's 100,000th payphone (ah, happy days), it was opened by Sir Ranulph Fiennes. Of course.

And please note that this is another campsite for which avid GPSers should take the postcode with a pinch of salt (it will take you off to Brunghill Farm, a mile up the road).

Ship Inn
Piel Island
Barrow-in-Furness
Cumbria
LA13 0QN

Steve and Sheila Chattaway
07516 453784
shipinn@pielisland.co.uk
www.pielisland.co.uk
Landranger: 96 (SD 232 637)

THE BASICS
Size: ⁹/₁₀ acre.
Pitches: Variable (0 hardstanding).
Terrain: Flat.
Shelter: To south.
View: Barrow, the Lake District, the Fylde coastline.
Waterside: A freshwater pool, plus the Irish Sea and Piel Channel.
Electric hook-ups: No.
Noise/Light/Olfactory pollution: No.

THE FACILITIES
Loos: 2M 3W & pub toilets: 1M 2W.
Showers: 1M 1W (cold water only). Plans for 1M 1W with hot water (all free).
Other facilities: No.
Stuff for children: No.
Recycling: No.

THE RULES
Dogs: On leads.
Fires: No open fires; BBQs off grass.
Other: No.

PUB LIFE
The Ship Inn (free house) opening hours 'flexible' 7D; food served Tue–Sun 8.30am–7pm.

SHOP
Co-op, Roose Road, Roose (4 miles from Roa Island) – small supermarket; open 7am–10pm 7D; 01229 822730.

THERE AND AWAY
Train station: Roose (4 miles from Roa Island) – Barrow-in-Furness to Lancaster line. **Ferry**: Piel Island Ferry runs from Roa Island from 11am to 5pm, weather

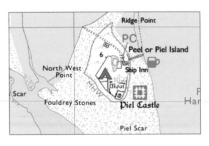

permitting; adult £4 return, U14 £2, U4 free; contact John Cleasby 07798 794550 or Steve Chattaway 07516 453784.

OUT AND ABOUT
Furness Abbey, Barrow-in-Furness (5¾ miles from Roa Island) – the majestic ruins of an abbey founded in 1123 by Stephen, Count of Blois (later to become King Stephen); adult £3.50, child £1.80; open daily July to August, April to June & September Thur–Mon 10am–5pm, October to March w/es only 10am–4pm; 01229 823420; www.english-heritage.org.uk.
Walney Island (1½ miles at low tide) – 'wet and windy Walney' has 2 large nature reserves and is home to the largest colony of lesser black-backed and herring gulls in Europe; www.walney-island.com.
The Dock Museum, Barrow (6 miles from Roa Island) – an innovative museum of local life inside a former dry dock; free; open Easter to October Tue–Fri 10am–5pm, w/es & BH 11am–5pm (last admission 4.15pm); November to Easter Wed–Fri 10.30am–4pm, w/es 11am–4.30pm (last admission 3.45pm); 01229 876400; www.dockmuseum.org.uk.

open	All year
tiny campsites' rating	★★★
friendliness	☺ ☺ ☺
cost	BP £, Couple £, Family £

CUMBRIA

There's something about Piel Island. Accessible only via a tiny ferry or a mile-and-a-half low-tide walk over the sands from Walney Island, its 52 acres comprise one medieval castle, one pub (whose landlord is recognised as the King of Piel), one brief terrace of Victorian houses, some grassland, a population of 'four, sometimes five' and a beach. Oh, and, of course, in 1487 it was the scene of the last invasion of Great Britain.

While camping is allowed almost anywhere on the island, there are two 'official' campsites – a field behind the pub and a patch ironically named 'The Crescent' (it's not a natural slice of suburb). The latter is in a slight dip and protected by shrubs, which help divert the Atlantic winds. The view from either is astonishing: a vista that stretches all the way from Lake District hills across Morecambe Bay, and along the Fylde Coast to Blackpool Tower.

The pub, the Ship Inn, reopened in 2010 following a major renovation and campers propping up the bar of an evening supping a locally brewed beer can expect to be joined by sundry stray kayakers and yachters. King Steve is not only the landlord but a trained chef – his halloumi and sweet pepper wraps are especially delicious.

The castle is permanently open and free. It started life as a wool store, which, when constructed by monks in the 12th century, was the second largest building in Britain after the Tower of London.

Do consult Steve before attempting the crossing from Walney (possible for about four hours every day). Alternatively, local guide and nature expert John Murphy will take groups across (01229 473746).

THE CRESCENT

Blawith
Ulverston
Cumbria
LA12 8EW

Mrs Linda Nicholson
01229 885277
info@birchbank.co.uk
www.birchbank.co.uk
OS Landranger: 96 (SD 261 875)

THE BASICS
Size: 9/10 acre.
Pitches: 20 (1 hardstanding).
Terrain: Very gently sloping.
Shelter: Yes.
View: Great Burney and other hills to the south; the Woodland Fells to the north.
Waterside: Smithy beck.
Electric hook-ups: 8.
Noise/Light/Olfactory pollution: No.

THE FACILITIES
Loos: 3U. **Showers**: 3U (free; inc. family room with loo & shower).
Other facilities: Washing-up area, washing machine, tumble-dryer, fridge/freezer, CDP.
Stuff for children: Building dams in the beck.
Recycling: Everything.

THE RULES
Dogs: On leads on fells (sheep).
Fires: No open fires; BBQs off grass (2 BBQs available).
Other: No noise after 10pm.

PUB LIFE
The Farmers Arms (Scottish and Newcastle), Lowick Green (3¾ miles) – a bar and restaurant and 'probably the oldest inn in the Lakes'; open Mon 5–11pm, Tue–Sun 12–11pm; food served Mon 5–9pm, Tue 12–2pm & 5–9pm, Wed–Sun 12–9pm; 01229 861277; www.farmersarmslowick.co.uk.

SHOP
Grizebeck Filling Station (3½ miles) – extremely basic supplies; Mon–Fri 8am–7pm, w/es 9am–6pm; 01229 889259. Also

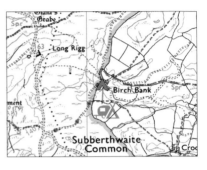

a small selection of shops in Greenodd and Broughton-in-Furness (both 5 miles).

THERE AND AWAY
Train station: Kirkby-in-Furness (5½ miles) – Barrow-in-Furness to Carlisle line. No onward bus service to the site.

OUT AND ABOUT
The Old Man of Coniston (Coniston start 8½ miles) – 803 metres of classic Lakeland fell. **Beacon Tarn** (1¾ miles) can be reached along footpaths, and the **Cumbria Way** (bit.ly/o3KIKS) followed without touching an inch of road. **Coniston** – both the town (8½ miles) and the lake (3¾ miles at Lake Bank) are well worth a visit. John Ruskin's home, **Brantwood** (01539 441396; www.brantwood.org.uk) is best reached by taking the steam yacht *Gondola* (01539 432733; NT site) from Coniston Quay; while the **Ruskin Museum** (01539 441164; www.ruskinmuseum.com) also covers speedster Donald Campbell and his ill-fated Bluebird; bit.ly/tnqM7u.

open	Mid May to October
tiny campsites' rating	★ ★
friendliness	☺ ☺ ☺
cost	BP ££, Couple £££, Family £££

Travel three or four miles inland from the Cumbrian coast, turn left off the main road and, coming over the top of a rise, there's suddenly nothing between you and the Lakeland Fells but a single long valley. Tucked under those same hills is Birchbank Farm, halfway along a picturesque road to pretty much nowhere (unless, I suppose, you live in the farm at the very end).

Set alongside the sheds on this 500-acre sheep and cattle farm, the campsite meanders gracefully down to a small stream called Smithy beck and onto the flat parts of a field just the other side. There are free-range eggs for sale and, for a farm site, an unusually wide spread of facilities on offer. The washing machine, tumble-dryer and family loo/shower room make it especially attractive to people who are introducing their children to the delights of outdoor holidays.

The views of the surrounding hills are, of course, a constant enticement to get out and walk them. Perhaps the greatest draw comes from the Old Man of Coniston to the north, from whose summit Morecambe Bay, Blackpool Tower and even the Isle of Man can be glimpsed given a clear day. If your hiking horizons are a shade less ambitious, pick up one of the printed maps available on site. These mark out an easy circular walk to the remains of an ancient settlement nearby.

If you're up for a day by the coast, Kirkby-in-Furness and the delights of the Cumbria Coastal Way (bit.ly/tQSPqM) are just five miles away.

Dalegarth Guest House
Hassness Estate
Buttermere
Cumbria
CA13 9XA

James and Kelly Gillings
01768 770233
dalegarthhouse@hotmail.co.uk
www.dalegarthguesthouse.co.uk
Landranger: 89 (NY 186 159)

THE BASICS
Size: ⅖ acre.
Pitches: 35 (1 hardstanding).
Terrain: Flat terraces.
Shelter: Yes.
View: No.
Waterside: 2 minutes' walk from Lake Buttermere.
Electric hook-ups: No.
Noise/Light/Olfactory pollution: No.

THE FACILITIES
Loos: 2M 3W. **Showers**: 1M 1W (50p for '6 min.').
Other facilities: Fridge/freezer, phone-charger socket, drying room, social room with pool table, darts etc.
Stuff for children: Rope swings, woods, fairy glades.
Recycling: Glass, tins, plastics.

THE RULES
Dogs: Under control (sheep about).
Fires: Open fires in fire baskets; slate available for BBQs (covered BBQ area at foot of site). **Other**: No.

PUB LIFE
A short walk along the lakeside brings you to Buttermere village and the **Bridge Hotel** – a rather swish affair; open Mon–Sat 9am–11pm, Sun till 10.30pm; food served 9am–9.30pm 7D; 01768 770252; www.bridge-hotel.com. Still rather nice, but not quite so swish or pricey, is the **Fish Hotel**; open April to September 10.30am–10.30pm 7D, October to March shorter hours (see website) and closed Tue–Wed; food served 12–2pm & 6–9pm 7D; 01768 770253; www.fishinnbuttermere.co.uk.

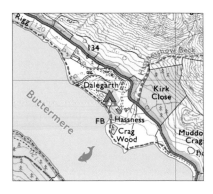

SHOP
Basic foodstuffs (milk and bread etc.) and camping equipment can be bought on site. Otherwise, there are shops aplenty in Keswick (9 miles).

THERE AND AWAY
Train station: Maryport (18 miles) – Carlisle to Barrow-in-Furness line. No direct bus to Dalegarth from Maryport, but bus nos. 77 & 77A (Honister Rambler) run from Keswick to Buttermere from April to October.

OUT AND ABOUT
Honister Slate Mine's *Via ferrata*
(5¼ miles) – the 'iron way' is a route of supports in the rock face that can be climbed while safely attached to a cable: an exhilarating method once used by miners here; adult £30, child (10–15) £20, family £95; daily 9am, noon & 3pm; 01768 777714. Fell walking – **Scafell Pike**, **Pillar** and **Haystacks** (Wainwright's favourite) are all within easy reach.

open	March to October
tiny campsites' rating	★★
friendliness	☺ ☺ ☺
cost	BP ££, Couple £££, Family ££££

Buttermere was Alfred Wainwright's favourite lake, and anyone who has had even a minute's acquaintance with it will understand why. It's a comparatively small stretch of water by Lake District standards, but the reflection of the hills in its placid waters screams out to be photographed and stuck on the lid of a really expensive tin of shortbread biscuits.

There are very few properties on Buttermere's shores, making Dalegarth even more of a find. In woodland below the lakeside road, the sloping terrain has been transformed into three terraces of level camping ground, just a two-minute walk through trees to the shore, where one of the tastiest views imaginable awaits. Children are free to run around and play in the grounds, where they will find rope swings and fairy glades in the woods.

The site (and attached B&B) was taken over in 2009 by James and Kelly, a young couple brimming over with enthusiasm and ideas. They've converted one of the garages at the top of the site into a wet-weather hangout for campers, with sofas, games and other little luxuries to make the wait for blue skies a cheerier affair. They can also supply sandwiches, flapjacks and hot drinks throughout the day; and packed lunches for whatever expedition you see fit to embark upon.

At night, the two pubs in the village of Buttermere lie a gorgeous 15-minute shoreline stroll away, past fluffy grey Herdwick sheep.

2 Rose Cottages
Studley Roger
Ripon
Yorkshire
HG4 3AY

Dave Jelley and Damaris Armstrong
01765 603506 & 07969 260858
info@jelleylegs.co.uk
www.jelleylegs.co.uk
Landranger: 99 (SE 289 702)

THE BASICS
Size: 1/50 acre.
Pitches: 2 (0 hardstanding).
Terrain: Flattish lawn.
Shelter: All round.
View: Field and Studley Royal Park beyond.
Waterside: No
Electric hook-ups: No.
Noise/Light/Olfactory pollution: The friendly chatter of birds, including geese, curlews and tawny owls.

THE FACILITIES
Loos: 1U **Showers**: 1U (new wetroom; free).
Other facilities: Veggie breakfast/dinner (£5/£10) served in the kitchen; in wet weather, owners offer 'sleeping bags on beds for £15pp' B&B (if beds available).
Stuff for children: A swing on a tree, huge fields a short car-free walk away.
Recycling: Everything.

THE RULES
Dogs: Under control.
Fires: Only in fire wok (free fuel provided).
Other: Quiet after 11pm. Children to be supervised near the pond.

PUB LIFE
The Royal Oak (Timothy Taylor), Ripon (1½ miles) – a former coaching inn serving posh nosh; open Mon–Fri 11am–11pm, Sat till midnight, Sun 12–10.30pm; food served Mon–Fri 12–2.30pm & 5.30–9pm (Fri till 9.30pm), Sat 12–9.30pm, Sun 12–7pm; 01765 602284; www.royaloakripon.co.uk.

SHOP
Booths, Ripon (1½ miles) – think Waitrose but with a northern twang; open

Mon–Sat 8am–8pm, Sun 9.30am–4pm; 01765 698540; www.booths.co.uk.

THERE AND AWAY
Train station: Thirsk/Harrogate (10/12 miles). Dave can pick up campers from both (£10 single, £15 return). Bus no. 70 runs from Thirsk to Ripon, no. 36 runs from Harrogate to Ripon, 1½ miles from the site.

OUT AND ABOUT
Fountains Abbey (1 mile) – stunning abbey ruins in landscaped grounds with the Studley Royal Deer Park attached; adult £8.15, child £4.40, family £20.90; open daily April to September 10am–5pm, (see website for rest of year), deer park open all year during daylight hours; 01765 608888; www.fountainsabbey.org.uk.

open	All year
tiny campsites' rating	★ ★ ★
friendliness	☺ ☺ ☺
cost	BP ££, Couple ££££, Family ££££

There's an old Chinese proverb (they're always old – one rather wishes the Chinese would get around to making up some new ones) that claims, 'If you would be happy your whole life long, become a gardener.' If you don't have a garden, however, there's no need to fret because you can come and stay in this beautiful North Yorkshire one and at least be happy for the bit of your life you spend here.

There's room for just two tents, making it possibly the tiniest campsite in the land, in one of its smallest villages (sneeze and you'll miss Studley Roger). Cramped, however, it is not. Behind the trees, shrubs and floral delights stands a field of waving wheat.* Behind the field is a deer park, and behind the deer park is Fountains Abbey, a 12th-century ruin in 18th-century landscaped gardens, and a UNESCO World Heritage site to boot. Turn in the opposite direction and you'll see Ripon, the three towers of its cathedral a beacon for those making the journey across the fields to the miniature city's pubs and restaurants.

Dave and Damaris offer delicious Aga-cooked vegetarian breakfasts and evening meals straight from the pages of a huge Ottolenghi cookbook.

And should you feel the need to build up an appetite worthy of the dishes, Dave (an ultra-marathon runner) organises two-night breaks on which you can improve your long-distance running technique (or pick one up if you don't already have one). If you prefer two wheels to two feet, you're perfectly placed for the Way of the Roses, the new coast-to-coast cycle path, which passes right by the front door.

*Crops may change from year to year. Waving not guaranteed.

Holmpton
Withernsea
Yorkshire
HU19 2QR

Mike and Kath Cox
01964 630957
OS Landranger: 107 (TA 365 232)

THE BASICS
Size: ⅓ acre.
Pitches: Variable (room for 5 caravans and 5 tents; 1 hardstanding).
Terrain: Flat.
Shelter: Yes.
View: The lights of Withernsea at night from farmyard.
Waterside: No.
Electric hook-ups: 6.
Noise/Light/Olfactory pollution: Light outside loo; the occasional neigh.

THE FACILITIES
Loos: 1U. **Showers**: 1U (50p – no time limit – pay on departure).
Other facilities: Washing-up sink; road bikes for hire (£1.50/hour).
Stuff for children: No.
Recycling: Everything.

THE RULES
Dogs: Under control at all times (horses around). **Fires**: No open fires; BBQs off grass. **Other**: No.

PUB LIFE
The George and Dragon (free house), Holmpton (50 metres) – quiz night last Friday of the month; open Mon–Sat 12–2pm & 5pm–'everyone's gone home' (licenced to 2am), Sun 12–'everyone's gone home'; food served Mon–Sat 12–2pm & 5–8pm (Fri & Sat till 9pm), Sun 12–8pm; 01964 630478.

SHOP
Costcutter, Patrington (3 miles) – convenience store; open Mon–Sat 6.30am–8pm, Sun 7.30am–7pm; 01964

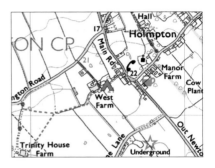

631315. There's a wide selection of shops along the coast at Withernsea (3½ miles).

THERE AND AWAY
Train station: Hull (20 miles) – a terminus for various lines. From Hull, take bus no. 75/77/175 (www.eyms.co.uk) to Withernsea, then hop on no. 71/71A (same company) to Holmpton.

OUT AND ABOUT
RAF Holmpton (300 metres) – a huge cold war underground nuclear bunker with café and cheery weapons of mass destruction gallery; adult £6, child £5, family (2+3) £19; tour (2.30pm) most days from March to October; 01964 630208; www.rafholmpton.com.
Spurn Head (10 miles) – an extraordinary 3½-mile spit of land shooting out into the Humber Peninsula, owned by Yorkshire Wildlife Trust – thousands of migrant birds and winter visitors land here, making it a magnet for birders; free (£3/car); always open; 01904 659570; www.ywt.org.uk/reserves/spurn-nature-reserve.

open	All year
tiny campsites' rating	★
friendliness	☺ ☺
cost	BP ££, Couple ££, Family ££

This is unnervingly impermanent country. Villages around here have flourished, only to find themselves swallowed up by the sea. The fantastically named Ravenser Odd, for instance, which had its own MP and everything, now languishes under the waves a full mile-and-a-half offshore. There's something reassuringly solid, therefore, about Elmtree's Grade II-listed brick farmhouse. A small field around the back, its edges pleasingly tousled with hedge bindweed and house-trained nettles, has just enough shelter to make you feel snug without creating a sense of being hemmed in. The loo and shower, meanwhile, are part of the farm buildings, with easy access for campers.

The straggle of dwellings that makes up the unspoilt village of Holmpton is well worth a slow wander around. It is said to give a very good idea of what coastal settlements of times past would have looked like, and as such has been designated a Conservation Village. To see a number of really striking houses, take the more southerly of the two roads that lead straight out, for half a mile, to the sea. At the end, a footpath leads to cliffs above a long and (almost always) deserted sandy beach sweeping around to Withernsea, a small town three miles away along a cliff-top path.

The George and Dragon pub, being so close, serves as a useful annex to one's tent in bad weather and rustles up very economical bar meals as well as doing takeaways, particularly welcome after cycling the 46-mile National Byway loop (www.thenationalbyway.org) that passes through the village.

45 Wold Farm

Bempton Lane
Flamborough
Bridlington
Yorkshire
YO15 1AT

David Southwell
01262 850536
woldfarmcamping@live.com
www.woldfarmcampsite.tk
OS Landranger: 101 (TA 217 722)

THE BASICS
Size: ⅔ acre.
Pitches: Variable (0 hardstanding).
Terrain: Pretty flat.
Shelter: On south and west.
View: Over fields to the sea.
Waterside: No, but just 400 metres from the sea.
Electric hook-ups: No.
Noise/Light/Olfactory pollution: A movement-sensitive light on the way to the loo; occasional braying.

THE FACILITIES
Loos: 2U. **Showers**: No.
Other facilities: CDP.
Stuff for children: Donkeys and sheep to stroke and feed.
Recycling: No.

THE RULES
Dogs: On leads and allowed at owners' discretion. **Fires**: No open fires; BBQs off grass (bricks available). **Other**: No.

PUB LIFE
There are a dozen or so pubs in and around Flamborough, but the most highly recommended is the **Rose & Crown** (free house), High Street; open noon–midnight 7D; food served 12–8pm; 01262 850455.

SHOP
Co-op, Flamborough (1¼ miles) – small supermarket; open 7am–10pm 7D; 01262 850283.

THERE AND AWAY
Train station: Bempton (3 miles) – Scarborough to Hull line. Bus no. 510

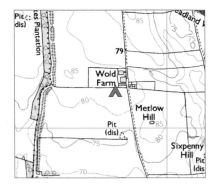

(www.eyms.co.uk) from Bridlington runs to Flamborough.

OUT AND ABOUT
Bempton Cliffs Cruise, North Pier, Bridlington (5 miles) – puffins from late May to mid July, skuas in September; adult £18, child (U14) £9, family £45; selected Saturdays and Sundays 9am, advance booking advised; 01262 850959; www.rspb.org.uk/datewithnature.
Flamborough Head Lighthouse (3 miles) – built in 1806 and still very flashy today; adult £3.10, U16 £2.10, family £10; open April to September (not Friday), 12–4pm, rest of year selected weekends only; 01262 673769; bit.ly/o7eusC.
South Landing Heritage/Sculpture Trail, nr Flamborough (2 miles) – a mile-long walk through a nature reserve peppered with playful sculptures; free; always open; bit.ly/r1iJlc.

open	All year
tiny campsites' rating	★ ★
friendliness	☺ ☺ ☺
cost	BP £££, Couple £££, Family £££

This is a site for lovers of open fields and big skies. Three-quarters of a mile up a rough track, Wold farmhouse stands in wondrous isolation on the great chalk promontory that is Flamborough Head. The camping field enjoys uninterrupted views over the sheep-filled fields to both Flamborough lighthouses (new one on the left, old one on the right) with a sliver of sea to top it off. There are just two loos and no shower, so this is not a place for luxury-seekers, but it's Eldorado for walkers and birdwatchers. Children too will enjoy the fact that they can stroke the farm's donkeys (including the elderly Bambi) and help feed the sheep.

Take the campsite's private footpath to the cliffs, just 400 metres away, and you can either birdwatch (puffins, gannets, skuas and countless others adorn the skies) or tackle the six-mile circular walk of the entire headland. Meanwhile, dipsomaniacs and those who just enjoy the odd tipple will be encouraged to learn that despite its apparently remote location, there are no fewer than 13 drinking establishments within a mile and a half of the site.

There are so many things to do in this corner of Yorkshire that the owners present campers with a welcome pack. It includes infomation on Sewerby Hall and Gardens (3 miles; 01262 673769), which has twice been voted Britain's Best Picnic Spot. Take along a sandwich and a flask (or a bottle of wine) and find out what all the fuss is about.

Kildale
Whitby
Yorkshire
YO21 2RN

Mr and Mrs D Cook
01642 722847
parkfarm_2000@yahoo.co.uk
www.kildalebarn.co.uk
OS Landranger: 94 (NZ 602 084)

THE BASICS
Size: ⅛ acre.
Pitches: Max. 30 people (0 hardstanding).
Terrain: Slopey.
Shelter: At foot of field.
View: West to the far-off Yorkshire Dales.
Waterside: No.
Electric hook-ups: No.
Noise/Light/Olfactory pollution:
Occasional bleating.

THE FACILITIES
Loos: 2U. **Showers**: 2U (£1 for 'about an hour').
Other facilities: Camping barn (sleeps 18; £7.50pp), tumble-dryer, picnic table.
Stuff for children: Can play in animal-free fields; bottle feeding of lambs on request.
Recycling: Everything.

THE RULES
Dogs: On leads.
Fires: No open fires; BBQs off grass.
Other: No.

PUB LIFE
The Dudley Arms (free house), Ingleby Greenhow (2½ miles by footpath and road) – 17th-century coaching inn with a bistro and restaurant; open Mon–Fri 12–3pm & 5–'late', w/es 12–'late'; food served Mon–Sat 12–2pm, 5–6.30pm (tea), 7–9.30pm (bistro & restaurant), Sun 12–2pm & 7–9.30pm; 01642 722526; www.dudleyarms.com.

SHOP
There is a good selection of shops and services in Great Ayton (4 miles) including a bakery, a greengrocers, an organic shop,

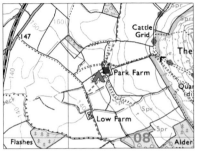

a café and a **Co-op** – small supermarket; open Mon–Sat 7am–10pm, Sun 8am–10pm; 01642 722219.

THERE AND AWAY
Train station: Kildale (1 mile) – Middlesbrough to Whitby line (aka the Esk Valley line). Then a mile's walk onward to the site.

OUT AND ABOUT
Cleveland Way (¾ mile) – 109-mile trail from Helmsley across the North York Moors to Filey, on the coast; 01439 770657; www.nationaltrail.co.uk/ClevelandWay.
Gisborough Priory, Guisborough (9¼ miles) – a ruined Augustinian priory from the 14th century with a mysterious missing 'u'; adult £1.80, child 90p, family £3.60; open April to September Tue–Sun 9am–5pm (rest of year open Wed–Sun); 01287 633801; www.english-heritage.co.uk.
Roseberry Topping (3 miles) – a 360-degree view from the top of the hill taking in Teeside through to the Yorkshire Dales; 01723 870423; NT site.

open	All year
tiny campsites' rating	★★★
friendliness	☺ ☺ ☺
cost	BP £, Couple ££, Family ££££

Location location location? So very yesterday. It's all about view view view. And Park Farm in Kildale enjoys one of the most sublime you'll ever find on these shores. It's roughly 50 miles west to Tan Hill and the Yorkshire Dales, and on a clear day you can see absolutely everything in between: a joyous swoop of fields, trees and yet more hills.

The campsite itself is a tiny soft-cheese-triangle of sloping grassland bordered on two sides by a low drystone wall, with a hawthorn hedge on the third. A few cooking-apple trees give some additional shelter (and added pectin to your diet if you time your visit right) particularly at the snug foot of the field. The site forms a very small part of a 700-acre farm populated by sheep and interesting cattle (fans of Limousin, Shorthorn, Charolais and Belgian Blue bring your spotter books).

Captain Cook was born and raised in these parts (scenes for a film about his life were shot on the farm) and a walk up to the Captain Cook monument on Easby Moor (1¾ miles) is highly recommended, if only for the astonishing photo opportunities.

Meanwhile, loos and showers are housed in one of the many handsome farm buildings close by. Next door, a fine-looking nearly windowless stone construction turns out to be a YHA camping barn (and a listed building to boot). Anywhere else and the heady mix of elevated sleeping quarters and flash fitted kitchen might tempt the camper inside. But then there's that view.

Bowbank
Middleton-in-Teesdale
County Durham
DL12 0NT

Richard and Stephanie Proud
01833 640135
richard@highsidefarm.co.uk
www.highsidefarm.co.uk
OS Landranger: 92 (NY 946 237)

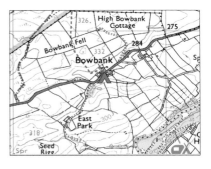

THE BASICS
Size: ¼ acre.
Pitches: Room for 8 people
(0 hardstanding).
Terrain: Mainly sloping.
Shelter: Some to the north.
View: North Pennines.
Waterside: No.
Electric hook-ups: 2.
Noise/Light/Olfactory pollution: No.

THE FACILITIES
Loos: 2U. **Showers**: 1U (free).
Other facilities: Washing-up room. Buy
Highside Farm-reared meat for the BBQ.
Stuff for children: No.
Recycling: Yes.

THE RULES
Dogs: On leads.
Fires: No open fires; BBQs off grass
(breeze blocks available).
Other: No visitors; departures before
noon; no arrivals before 1pm.

PUB LIFE
There are nearer pubs in Mickleton and
Middleton-in-Teesdale, but it's worth going
the extra mile or so to the **Three Tuns**
(free house) at Eggleston (4½ miles); open
Mon–Fri 11am–2.30pm & 6pm–midnight,
w/es 11am–midnight; food served
Mon–Sat 12–2pm & 6–9pm, Sun 12–9pm;
01833 650289; www.three-tuns-inn.co.uk.

SHOP
Co-op, Middleton-in-Teesdale (2 miles) –
small supermarket; open Mon–Sat 8am–
10pm, Sun 9am–8am; 01833 640860.
The town has a range of small shops too.

THERE AND AWAY
Train station: Kirkby Stephen (16 miles) –
Settle to Carlisle line. Or take bus no. 75/76
from Darlington to Barnard Castle and no.
95/96 from there to Middleton-in-Teesdale
(both www.arrivabus.co.uk).

OUT AND ABOUT
High Force Waterfall (9 miles by road
or 5 miles by footpath); adult £1.50, U16
free; 01833 640209. Or, for an even more
spectacular waterfall, there's **Cauldron
Snout**, 3 miles from the Cow Green
reservoir car park (11 miles) up the
Widdybank Fell nature trail (look out for
blue gentian and the Teesdale violet in
the spring); bit.ly/nCb6be.
Raby Castle, Staindrop (13 miles) –
a medieval castle and deer park as well
as the setting for the river pageant scene
in the film *Elizabeth*; ticket for castle, park
and gardens: adult £10, child (5–15)
£4.50, family £27; open Easter & May
to September (days vary according
to month); 01833 660202;
www.rabycastle.com.

open	May to September
tiny campsites' rating	★ ★
friendliness	☺ ☺ ☺
cost	BP ££, Couple ££££, Family £££££

As evening wears on, all that can be heard from Highside Farm's campsite, on the lower reaches of Lune Moor, is the sporadic bleating of sheep far away across the valley. As the light fades into night, our woolly friends fall silent and the sense of tranquillity is complete.

There's nothing rushed about Highside Farm. Many of the farm buildings date back to the 16th century or earlier, and while the owners, Richard and Stephanie, haven't turned the clock back quite that far, they have become subsistence farmers on their 16-acre smallholding: growing vegetables and tending four breeds of sheep (including the rare Teeswater), some pigs, cattle and chickens. They also spin their own wool, balls of which can be bought. Furthermore, if you order it the night before, they'll serve you a breakfast full of their own produce and locally sourced food.

An old stone shed has been transformed into two immaculate and homely loos, a shower and a washing-up room, while the campsite itself consists of one very small field with a static caravan just below it – perhaps the only visible concession to modernity – before the ground drops away rather dramatically, leaving nothing between you and the hills of the North Pennines to the south.

The Pennine Way (www.thepennineway.co.uk), perhaps understandably, rises near here by a rather less precipitous route and heads around the back of the farm, passing just half a mile away.

The Old Vicarage

Stotsfield Burn
Rookhope in Weardale
County Durham
DL13 2AE

Colin and Pauline Lomas
01388 517375
colin@finetime.wanadoo.co.uk
Landranger: 87 (NY 942 423)

THE BASICS
Size: ⅐ acre.
Pitches: Max. 20 people (0 hardstanding).
Terrain: More or less flat.
Shelter: All sides.
View: No.
Waterside: No.
Electric hook-ups: No.
Noise/Light/Olfactory pollution: No.

THE FACILITIES
Loos: 1U. **Showers:** 1U (free).
Other facilities: Outdoor washing-up area.
Stuff for children: No (it's not really a site geared up for children).
Recycling: Everything.

THE RULES
Dogs: At owners' discretion.
Fires: No open fires; BBQs at owners' discretion. **Other:** No cars except support vehicles and small vintage VW campervans; advance bookings preferred.

PUB LIFE
The Rookhope Inn (free house; ¼ mile) – a walker-/cyclist-friendly watering hole; open 11am–midnight 7D; food served 12–3pm & 6–9pm 7D; 01388 517215; www.rookhope.com.

SHOP
The shop with no name, Rookhope (¼ mile) – very basic stock indeed; open Mon–Wed & Sat 9am–noon, Thur till 10am, Fri till noon & 3–5pm. Otherwise, try the **Co-op**, Stanhope (5 miles) – small supermarket; open Mon–Sat 8am–10pm, Sun 9am–8pm; 01388 528219.

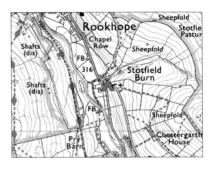

THERE AND AWAY
Train station: Hexham (18 miles) – Carlisle to Newcastle line. Bishop Auckland, on the Tees Valley line, is 22 miles away. From there, take bus no. 101 (Mon–Sat 8am–6pm, hourly; 01388 528235) to Stanhope, or do it in style by steam train (01388 526203; www.weardale-railway.org.uk). It's a scenic 4-mile hike from Stanhope to the site.

OUT AND ABOUT
C2C – the 140-mile cycle route starts at Whitehaven, finishes at Newcastle or Sunderland, and passes through Rookhope in Weardale at around mile 95; 08451 130065 (Sustrans); www.c2c-guide.co.uk.
Killhope, the North of England Lead Mining Museum, nr Cowshill (10 miles) – a multi-award-winning 19th-century lead mine and museum; 3-day pass for museum and mine: adult £7, child (4–16) £4, U4 free; open daily April to October 10.30am–5pm; 01388 537505; www.killhope.org.uk.

open	Easter to October
tiny campsites' rating	★ ★
friendliness	☺ ☺
cost	BP ££, Couple £££, Family £££££

Any cyclist or walker who has ever detected a smug look on the face of a passing car driver on a particularly draining hill, as the heavens have opened, finally gets to have the last laugh here, for this is a site dedicated to those getting around under their own steam. Thus, anyone thinking of rocking up here with a tent in the boot need not apply. The only circumstance in which a car will be allowed onto the driveway of The Old Vicarage is as a support vehicle for cyclists and walkers attempting a long-distance route (and then strictly one vehicle per team). As a concession to the petrol brigade, however (and because they look nice and owners Colin and Pauline used to have one themselves), small VW campervans are welcome.

The late-Victorian former vicarage is the possessor of a sort of wild lawn where feral plants outnumber blades of grass. This gives the camper the strange and far from unpleasant sensation of wild camping, while actually located in a garden – a sampling of the best of both worlds that is a rare privilege to be cherished.

Sadly, since the first edition of *Tiny Campsites* was published, the site's rampaging hen Matilda is no more, but is doubtless hassling St Peter for tidbits. However, the eventide candles on the tables are still present, giving the site an undeniably romantic air, and if you happen to arrive too exhausted to put your tent up, you can always ask if there's a bed free in the vicarage, where they do B&B.

49 Rye Hill Farm

Slaley
Hexham
Northumberland
NE47 0AH

Elizabeth Courage
01434 673259
info@ryehillfarm.co.uk
www.ryehillfarm.co.uk
Landranger: 87 (NY 958 579)

THE BASICS
Size: ⅜ acre.
Pitches: Variable (0 hardstanding).
Terrain: Ironing-board flat.
Shelter: On all sides.
View: Through the trees to hills and forests.
Waterside: No.
Electric hook-ups: 5.
Noise/Light/Olfactory pollution: No.

THE FACILITIES
Loos: 2U. **Showers**: 1U (free).
Other facilities: CDP.
Stuff for children: No.
Recycling: Everything.

THE RULES
Dogs: On leads.
Fires: No open fires; BBQs off grass.
Other: Pre-booking advisable.

PUB LIFE
Travellers Rest (free house), Slaley (not in the village, but on the B6306 towards Hexham; ¾ mile) – beer garden; open 12–11pm 7D; food served Mon–Sat 12–3pm & 5–9pm, Sun 12–3pm; 01434 673231; www.travellersrestslaley.com.

SHOP
The Village Shop, Slaley (1 mile) – milk, bread, newspapers and other basics (Margaret, the owner, has been behind the till for over 40 years and has received an MBE for her service); open Mon–Fri 9am–1pm, Sat 9am–12.30pm, Sun till noon; 01434 673201.

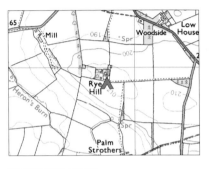

THERE AND AWAY
Train station: Hexham (5 miles) – Carlisle to Newcastle line. Bus no. 689 (www.simplygo.com) goes from Hexham to Slaley a few times a day.

OUT AND ABOUT
Chesters Roman Fort, Hadrian's Wall (10 miles) – Britain's best-preserved Roman cavalry fort; adult £5, child £3; open daily late March to September 10am–6pm; October to late March 10am–4pm; 01434 681379; www.english-heritage.org.uk.
Beamish Open Air Museum (21 miles) – a museum that takes the novel approach of telling the story of the people of north-east England by homing in on 2 years: 1825 and 1913; adult £16, child (5–16) £10, family £46, (ticket prices may go up imminently; in winter, prices are reduced during weekdays because fewer sections of the museum are open); open daily April to October 10am–5pm (last admission 3pm), November to March Tue/Wed/Thur/Sat/Sun 10am–4pm (last admission 3pm); 01913 704000; www.beamish.org.uk.

open	Easter to October Half Term
tiny campsites' rating	★ ★
friendliness	☺
cost	BP ££, Couple ££, Family ££

Northumberland, a strikingly beautiful county, can also be an inhospitable one at times. The people are lovely, of course, but the combination of the occasionally quite vigorous weather (as bemoaned by Roman soldiers on Hadrian's Wall in a million letters home to sunny Italy) and the austere landscape have lent the place a reputation as a wild, and sometimes desolate, region. This all makes Rye Hill Farm something of a surprise, because although it's set up high enough to command views around the countryside, its campsite is not some wind-blown wasteland, but a pleasant treelined area with grass so diligently tended as to tempt one to call it a lawn.

A long driveway from the road through the 30-acre farm ensures that the only noise disturbing campers is the hearty bleating of sheep and, since the owners don't like the site to get too crowded, it's unlikely you'll be unduly disturbed by fellow campers from your contemplation of Slaley Forest, a couple of miles off to the south. Meanwhile, the free-range chickens that saunter around the campsite give the place an added air of rural charm and rusticity.

Walkers have any number of footpaths and tracks to choose from in the locality, out to Blanchland Moor, the Derwent Reservoir and the woods of Dipton and Slaley. A little further afield, Hadrian's Wall beckons. Chesters Roman Fort is the closest highlight, with its wonderful Victorian museum bursting with Roman artefacts, though none of those mournful letters home.

Banks
Brampton
Cumbria
CA8 2JH

David and Elizabeth Harding
01697 72538
elizabeth.harding@btinternet.com
www.quarryside.co.uk
OS Landranger: 86 (NY 569 646)

THE BASICS
Size: ⅓ acre
Pitches: 25 (0 hardstanding)
Terrain: Level and sloping pitches.
Shelter: Shelter from all sides but east.
View: Fields towards Birdoswald Fort.
Waterside: No.
Electric hook-ups: No.
Noise/Light/Olfactory pollution: Cows shuffling and mumbling quietly (in French) in the field next door.

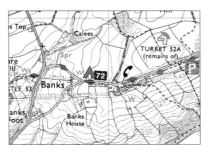

THE FACILITIES
Loos (portaloo): 1U. **Showers**: No (£2 to use wetroom in house).
Other facilities: Full English breakfast with local ingredients (£6), packed lunch (£5) – book both the night before. Free-range eggs for sale. B&B and holiday cottage.
Stuff for children: No.
Recycling: Glass, paper, cans.

THE RULES
Dogs: Under strict supervision.
Fires: No open fires; there's a large BBQ oil drum (charcoal £5/bag). **Other**: No.

PUB LIFE
The Belted Will Inn, Hallbankgate (5 miles) – a nickname given to Lord William Howard by Sir Walter Scott; in the *Good Beer Guide* too; open Mon–Fri 5pm–midnight, w/es noon–midnight; food served Mon–Fri 6.30–9pm, w/es 12–3pm & 6–9pm; 01697 746236. Site owners will drive guests to pub at 7pm and can pick them up later.

SHOP
Co-op, Brampton (4 miles) – small supermarket; open Mon–Fri 8am–5.30pm,

Sat till 1pm, Sun 9am–noon; 01697 746323. Lanercost (see below) has a very small farm shop. Milk, bread, beans and so forth can be bought from site owners.

THERE AND AWAY
Train station: Brampton (4 miles) – Newcastle to Carlisle line. The summer-only AD122 bus (see what they've done there?) runs between Newcastle and Carlisle via Brampton and Banks (01434 322002; bit.ly/nWkJMB)

OUT AND ABOUT
Hadrian's Wall – walking the 84-mile path is one of England's great life-enhancing experiences, with Birdoswald Fort the nearest major landmark; adult £5, child £3; open daily April to September 10am–5.30pm (see website for other times); 01697 747602; www.english-heritage.org.uk.
Lanercost Priory (1½ miles) – medieval church in top nick, with a tea room and farm shop; adult £3.30, child £2; open daily April to September 10am–5pm, (tea room & shop hours, see www.lanercosttearoom.co.uk); www.english-heritage.org.uk.

open	Easter to October
tiny campsites' rating	★ ★
friendliness	☺ ☺ ☺
cost	BP £, Couple ££, Family ££££

The Emperor Hadrian: traveller, philhellenist, deathbed poet – and the brains behind one of the largest proofs ever constructed that human beings don't always get along with one another. Considering that the wall was ostensibly built to mark the north-western limit of the Roman Empire and keep the dastardly Picts from raiding, it's intriguing to note that there are lots of places along it where the defences face south, suggesting that the Romans weren't picky when deciding who their enemies were.

Stay at Quarryside and you can give yourself a taste of what it must have been like to be a soldier on Hadrian's Wall, albeit that the locals are a good deal friendlier nowadays. The sliver of treelined field in the tiny village of Banks is a literal stone's throw from the site of the wall and, indeed, any stones you may find here might conceivably have once been part of the late Emperor's cordon sanitaire. The facilities are appropriately basic: just a (spectacularly clean) portaloo, picnic tables and a beautiful oil-drum barbecue made by co-owner David. Modern Invaders from the continent in the shape of Blonde d'Aquitaine cattle mooch about companionably in the field next door.

Your nearest wall action, Banks Turret, is a bare three-minute walk away and its eye-easing views over various ranges of fells can hardly have changed in the last couple of millennia. And should you crave even more impressive ruins, Birdoswald Roman Fort makes its defiant stand just three miles to the east.

Wales

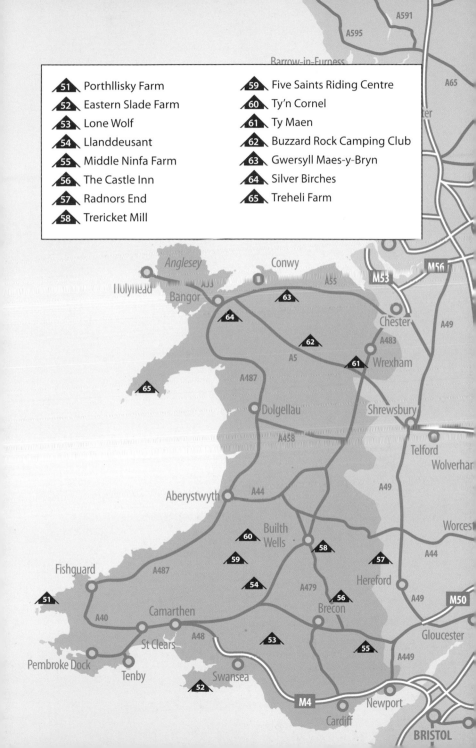

51	Porthllisky Farm	**59**	Five Saints Riding Centre
52	Eastern Slade Farm	**60**	Ty'n Cornel
53	Lone Wolf	**61**	Ty Maen
54	Llanddeusant	**62**	Buzzard Rock Camping Club
55	Middle Ninfa Farm	**63**	Gwersyll Maes-y-Bryn
56	The Castle Inn	**64**	Silver Birches
57	Radnors End	**65**	Treheli Farm
58	Trericket Mill		

St David's
Pembrokeshire
SA62 6RR

Robin Elliott
01437 720377
porthlisky.cott@btconnect.com (yep, just one 'l')
Landranger: 157 (SM 737 241)

THE BASICS
Size: ⁶/₇ acre.
Pitches: Variable (0 hardstanding).
Terrain: Flat.
Shelter: A low hedge on the western side.
View: Nearly 360 degrees.
Waterside: No.
Electric hook-ups: No.
Noise/Light/Olfactory pollution: No.

THE FACILITIES
Loos: No. **Showers**: No.
Other facilities: CDP.
Stuff for children: No.
Recycling: No.

THE RULES
Dogs: Under control.
Fires: At owner's discretion; BBQs
off grass.
Other: No.

PUB LIFE
Farmers Arms (free house), St David's
(1 mile) – friendly pub with beer garden;
open 11am–midnight 7D; food served
12–2.30pm & 6–9pm 7D; 01437 720328;
www.farmersstdavids.co.uk.

SHOP
St David's sports a range of mostly
small independent shops as well as
CK's (1½ miles), a large and rather funky
supermarket with a palindromic phone
number; open Mon–Sat 7am–10pm, Sun
10am–4pm; 01437 721127.

THERE AND AWAY
Train station: Haverfordwest (16 miles) –
Swansea to Milford Haven line. Bus no. 411

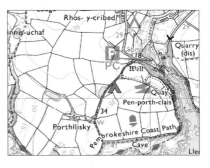

travels from the station to St David's, and
then it's a mile's walk to the site.

OUT AND ABOUT
St David's Cathedral (1 mile) – a place
of pilgrimage built on the site of a 6th-
century monastery whose steep grassy
grounds are just the spot on which to laze
with an ice cream in summer; free (guided
tour £4, booked in advance); open
daily 8.30am–5.30pm; 01437 720202;
www.stdavidscathedral.org.uk.
Pembrokeshire Coast Path (100 metres)
– from St Dogmaels in the north to Amroth
in the south, the trail comprises 186 miles
of spectacular coastline, cliffs, secret
coves, sandy beaches, small villages and
the occasional castle, the vast majority
of which lie within the Pembrokeshire
National Park; 08453 457275;
www.nt.pcnpa.org.uk.
St Non's Chapel (1¾ miles) – a holy well
and the ruins of the cliff-top chapel in
which St Non is said to have given birth
to David, who later became the patron
saint of Wales; bit.ly/pB2Poe.

open	All year
tiny campsites' rating	★ ★
friendliness	☺
cost	BP ££, Couple ££, Family ££

Never let it be said that the St David's Peninsula is short of a campsite or two. Indeed, sometimes it feels as if it's just one large campsite. Such is the area's popularity, finding a field that hasn't become a temporary village can be difficult, particularly in the school holidays. Happily, Porthllisky Farm, being much smaller than its counterparts and slightly off the beaten track, remains a little oasis of calm.

Indeed, despite being just a mile and a half from Britain's smallest city (pop. 1,800), just about the only sounds here come from passing gulls and the sighing sea. And then there's the view: a ring of mini mountains giving way to the stumpy tower of St David's cathedral.

The site is simplicity itself. Just under an acre of grass in a large open field on this potato-and-corn farm is mown to comfortable camping height. At one end there are some bins, while a water tap pokes out of a hedge. There are no loos, but 200 metres away at Porthclais Harbour (NT site) there are public conveniences that never seem to shut. There's also a very handy tiny café there that serves light refreshments outdoors, run by a very friendly chap called Steve (open daily May to September 10am–5pm 'and later if the weather's nice'; 07530 849078).

A special new path has been created through the farm to grant access to the nearby Pembrokeshire Coast Path, allowing campers to enjoy a spectacular one-day circular walk taking in the cliff-tops, a hill or two and St David's.

Oxwich
Gower
Swansea
SA3 1NA

Kate
☎ 01792 391374 & 07970 969814
tynrheol@hotmail.com
www.easternsladecampsite.freeservers.com
OS Landranger: 159 (SS 481 860)

THE BASICS
Size: ¾ acre (plus a small overspill strip for w/es and BHs in the summer).
Pitches: 20 tents and 5 campervans/caravans (0 hardstanding).
Terrain: Sloping.
Shelter: Low hedge all round but exposed to sea winds.
View: A fantastic seascape.
Waterside: No, but it's only a 10-minute walk to the sea.
Electric hook-ups: No.
Noise/Light/Olfactory pollution: No.

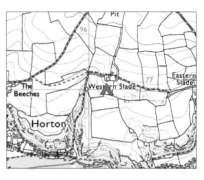

THE FACILITIES
Loos: 4U. **Showers**: No.
Other facilities: CDP.
Stuff for children: They can watch the cows being milked.
Recycling: Glass, tins.

THE RULES
Dogs: If well behaved.
Fires: 1 open fire in brazier; BBQs off grass.
Other: No.

PUB LIFE
Oxwich Bay Hotel (free house), Oxwich (1 mile) – the bar serves as the local pub and has a particularly pleasant and large beer garden (though they're a bit too posh to call it that); open Sun–Thur 8am–11pm, w/es till 10pm; food or bar snacks served throughout opening hours; 01792 390329; www.oxwichbayhotel.co.uk.

SHOP
General Stores (and tea shop), Oxwich (¾ mile) – very limited stock, but useful in an emergency; open February to October

8.30am–6pm 7D; 01792 391574. From November to January, or for a wider range of comestibles, try the shop at **Knelston petrol station** (4½ miles); open 7am–9pm 7D; 01792 390903.

THERE AND AWAY
Train station: Gowerton (13 miles) – Swansea to Milford Haven/Pembroke Dock line. In the summer, bus no. X18 (www.firstgroup.com) from Swansea stops ¼ mile from the site.

OUT AND ABOUT
Oxwich Castle, Oxwich (½ mile) – a stunning Tudor manor; adult £2.80, child £2.40, family £8; open daily April to September 10am–5pm; 01792 390359; www.cadw.wales.gov.uk.
Perriswood Archery and Falconry Centre, Penmaen (2½ miles) – birds of prey and outdoor archery (indoors if wet); 1-hour archery lesson £14, various packages available; open daily 10am–7pm; 01792 371661; www.perriswoodarchery.com.

open	Easter to October
tiny campsites' rating	★ ★ ★
friendliness	☺ ☺ ☺
cost	BP ££, Couple ££, Family £££

There's been a campsite in this field on the Gower Peninsula for 60 years, and there are no prizes for guessing why. High above Port Eynon Bay (the climb up from Oxwich is not for the faint of leg), Eastern Slade Farm commands tremendous views across the Bristol Channel to Ilfracombe and Hartland Point in Devon. Even far-off Lundy can be seen on a clear day: look along Port Eynon Point to the Helwick marker, whose bell rings dolefully out in misty weather, and the island is beyond it on the horizon.

However, it's not just the views that make this a great campsite. For all their protestations that they are 'dairy farmers first and campsite owners second', the owners are extraordinarily sociable. They are often to be found around a fire of an evening offering an open invitation for campers to join them for a bottle of beer or a glass of wine. Their conviviality tends to rub off on all who visit, making this definitely not the sort of site where people use windbreaks to stake out their own personal fiefdom.

The rocky shoreline at Slade Bay is a 10-minute stroll away down grassy paths. The rockpooling opportunities are excellent and, most unusually for the Gower, the beach is gratifyingly underpopulated since it seems to be patronised only by those using the campsite.

The field is quite sloped, so be prepared to Velcro your sleeping mat to your groundsheet or put into action whatever other tactic you employ for such conditions; while four portaloos are the sum total of the facilities, but everyone seems to like it that way.

Glyn y Mul Farm
Aberdulais
Neath
SA10 8HF

Ian Wyndgarde
01639 643204
glynymulfarm@btconnect.com
(recommended means of booking)
www.lonewolfcampsite.co.uk
OS Landranger: 170 (SN 782 011)

THE BASICS
Size: 1 acre.
Pitches: 20 in woodland (0 hardstanding).
Terrain: All sorts.
Shelter: In woods.
View: No.
Waterside: The River Dulais.
Electric hook-ups: No.
Noise/Light/Olfactory pollution: The rush and gush of the river.

THE FACILITIES
Loos: 1M 1W 3U. **Showers**: 2U (free).
Other facilities: Washroom; kitchen with fridge, microwave, toaster, kettle, washing-up area; CDP.
Stuff for children: No.
Recycling: Everything.

THE RULES
Dogs: Under strict supervision (sheep on farm). **Fires**: In woodland with moveable stone circles (firewood £5/sack).
Other: No music (apart from the odd acoustic guitar).

PUB LIFE
Rock and Fountain (free house), Aberdulais (1½ miles) – runs a free minibus service to the campsite for patrons; open 11am–11pm 7D; food served 12–9pm; 01639 642681. At time of going to print the **Dulais Rock Inn** (¾ mile) was being refurbished (you can ask Ian if it has reopened).

SHOP
Ella's Store, Aberdulais (1 mile) – very small shop stocking basics; open Mon–Fri 8.15am–8pm, Sat 9am–1.30pm & 4–8pm, Sun 10am–1.30pm & 4–7pm.

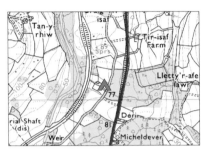

THERE AND AWAY
Train station: Neath (5 miles) – London to Swansea line. A taxi from the station to the site typically costs £10 – Ian can give tel no.

OUT AND ABOUT
Aberdulais Falls (1½ miles) – glorious waterfalls and some industrial history on the side, as well as the largest electricity-generating waterwheel in Europe; adult £4.05, child £2.02, family £10.13; open daily end March to October 10am–5pm (see website for other times of year); 01639 636674; NT site.
Afan Forest Park (12 miles) – 5 world-class mountain bike trails – from the 9-mile 'White's Level' to the dramatic 28–mile 'Skyline' – that draw riders from all over Europe; www.afanforestpark.co.uk.

open	April to end September
tiny campsites' rating	★ ★ ★
friendliness	☺ ☺ ☺
cost	BP ££, Couple £££, Family ££££

You can come to the Lone Wolf campsite and stay on one of its two small 'normal' fields if you like. However, if you do you'd definitely be missing out, because it's the woods that are special here. Crossing a single-track railway (it's for freight use only and the line can go weeks without seeing a train), you enter a much wilder world. You can pitch your tent wherever you like among the ancient wood of Welsh oaks and yellow

archangels, by what was once a blue pennant stone quarry, but the most popular spots are those along the banks of the rushing River Dulais.

However, about one in five of the people who camp here don't even bring along a tent, preferring to string up a basha or tarp across the trees and sleep beneath it, thus getting as close to nature as it is possible to be, short of simply lying down in a bush and having birds make a nest in your hair. Building open fires and engaging in activities that have a back-to-nature feel to them are actively encouraged at this place.

Ian, the very friendly owner of the site, is a self-confessed 'recycling enthusiast', so many of the materials that have gone into the buildings that house the facilities first saw life elsewhere, which lends an esoteric pick 'n' mix feel to the place. Meanwhile, the loos, showers and kitchen are all just a short walk out of the woods, making it a perfect place to hone your wild camping skills, while having a few home comforts close to hand.

The Old Red Lion
Llanddeusant
Carmarthenshire
SA19 9UL

Paul Smith

08453 719750

llanddeusantmanager@yha.org.uk

yha.org.uk

OS Landranger: 160 (SN 776 245)

THE BASICS
Size: ⅟₁₇ acre.
Pitches: 10 (0 hardstanding).
Terrain: Flat/slightly sloping.
Shelter: Yes, except to west.
View: Garreg Llwyd and Coed Pen Arthur.
Waterside: No.
Electric hook-ups: No.
Noise/Light/Olfactory pollution: Lights from hostel (if any on).

THE FACILITIES
Loos: 1M 1W 1U. **Showers**: 2U (free).
Other facilities: Picnic tables, washing machine (pay by donation), drying room, lounge (with open fire), bike shed, bikes for hire (07576 431960), books, fully equipped kitchen (inc. microwave). NB The hostel is closed from 10am–5pm, though you may still pitch your tent.
Stuff for children: Board games, outdoor games (quoits, cricket set), small woodland garden and, nearby, a tiny copse.
Recycling: Everything (inc. compost).

THE RULES
Dogs: Yes (but not inside hostel). **Fires**: If the planned firepit is there, open fires – yes, otherwise – no; gas BBQ available; other BBQs off grass. **Other**: No.

PUB LIFE
Red Lion (Cariad Coaching Inns), Llangadog (6½ miles) – Evan Evans beers from nearby Llandeilo and a wide range of food; open 9am–11pm (may close earlier on quiet nights) 7D; food served Mon–Sat 11am–3pm & 6–9.30pm, Sun 11am–2.30pm & 5–8.30pm; 01550 777357; www.redlioncoachinginn.co.uk. **Farmyard**

Café, Blaenau Farm (1¼ miles) offers light refreshments (and evening meals if booked ahead); open 8am–7pm 7D; 01550 740277.

SHOP
LJ Bailey & Sons, Llangadog – convenience store; open Mon/Tue/Thur 7.30am–1pm & 2–5.30pm, Wed/Sat 7.30am–1pm, Fri 7.30am–1pm & 2–6pm; 01550 777217. Canned food and bicycle parts can also be bought from Paul, Llanddeusant's warden.

THERE AND AWAY
Train station: Llangadog (7 miles) – Shrewsbury to Swansea line (aka the Heart of Wales line). No onward bus service.

OUT AND ABOUT
Llyn y Fan Fach (2½ miles) – a glaciated lake below the high ledge of Waun Lefrith, reached by a narrow road and track (passing the Farmyard Café – see above).
Carreg Cennen Castle (8 miles) – castle ruins in a dramatic setting (take a torch to explore a cave); adult £4, child (5–16) £3.50, family £12; open daily 9.30am–5.30pm (summer) & 9.30am–4pm (winter); 01558 822291; www.carregcennencastle.com.

open	Easter to early September
tiny campsites' rating	★ ★ ★
friendliness	☺ ☺ ☺
cost	BP ££, Couple ££££, Family £££££

Once a drovers' watering hole called the Red Lion, this small terrace of cottages in the western Brecon Beacons changed from hostelry to hostel in 1949. By the looks of the small stone shed that used to act as the campers' loo, the campsite outside the hostel's front door goes back some years as well. These days, those spending the night on the handkerchief-sized patch of grass are graciously allowed to use the hostel's conveniences, and very spruce they are too.

Situated in the Fforest Fawr Geopark, on the northern foothills of the Black Mountain (singular – confuse it with the Black Mountains at your peril), getting to Llanddeusant requires a climb from whichever direction you attempt the approach. The reward – aside from a campsite out of mobile signal, but on both Beacons and Cambrian Ways – is a stonking view from your tent: the wide green carpet of the valley stretching out to the pleasing curves of far Garreg Llwyd.

Llanddeusant, as Welsh speakers will tell you if you ask nicely, means Church of Two Saints. Sadly, St Simon and St Jude are rarely seen in these parts nowadays, but their handsome house of worship is still here, just behind the hostel. Inside you'll usually find for sale some genuinely tasteful craftwork made by members of the congregation.

Meanwhile, at the Red Kite Feeding Centre (1¼ miles; redkiteswales.co.uk), the mighty raptors are fed daily at 3pm (in summer months). Non-raptors will be happy to learn that they can chow down themselves, at the centre's licensed café.

Llanellen
nr Abergavenny
Monmouthshire
NP7 9LE

Richard and Rohan Lewis
01873 854662
richard@middleninfa.co.uk
www.middleninfa.co.uk
Landranger: 161 (SO 285 115)

THE BASICS
Size: 1/24 acre.
Pitches: 3 (0 hardstanding). There are also 4 'remote' pitches further up the hill.
Terrain: Flat, but 1 pitch bumpy.
Shelter: Yes.
View: Vale of Usk and the Skirrid mountain.
Waterside: No.
Electric hook-ups: No.
Noise/Light/Olfactory pollution: No.

THE FACILITIES
Loos (compost): 2U. **Showers**: 1U (solar-heated and lit; free).
Other facilities: Wood-fired sauna (small charge), bunkhouse (sleeps 6), fruit & veg grown on site for sale (other local organic food can also be ordered in advance of your stay), laminated maps of local footpaths and a mountain bike route to borrow. **Stuff for children**: Tennis court, croquet lawn. **Recycling**: Everything.

THE RULES
Dogs: At owners' discretion (sheep, ducks and horses about). **Fires**: Open fires (wood £2.50/bag); BBQs off grass.
Other: No.

PUB LIFE
Lamb and Fox (free house), Pwlldu (4 miles) – only building left of an abandoned village, it's a low-ceilinged affair with open fire; open Fri 6.45–11pm, Sat 3–11pm, Sun and BH 12–10.30pm; food served Fri 7.30–9pm, Sat 3–9pm, Sun 12–6pm; 07790 682832. **Goose and Cuckoo** (free house), Upper Llanover (3 miles) – cosy award-winning country pub; open Tue–Thur 11.30am–3pm & 7–11pm, Fri–Sat 11.30am–

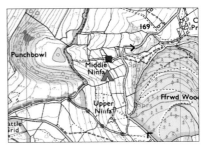

11pm, Sun 12–10.30pm; food served Tue–Sat 12–2.30pm & 7–8.30pm, Sun 12–2.30pm (no credit cards); 01873 880277; www.gooseandcuckoo.com. Maps showing routes to both pubs available on site.

SHOP
Llanellen Stores, Llanellen (2¼ miles) – convenience store, newspapers, off licence; open Mon–Fri 8.30am–5.30pm, Sat till 1pm; 01873 852530. Abergavenny (2½ miles) is a market town with a wide range of shops.

THERE AND AWAY
Train station: Abergavenny (2¾ miles) – Newport to Hereford line. It costs around £6 for a taxi from the station to the site; tell the driver to go the Llanfoist way.

OUT AND ABOUT
Big Pit, Blaenavon (5½ miles) – join an underground tour of the mine and discover what it was like to be a coal miner; free; open daily 9.30am–5pm (tours from 10am–3.30pm); 01495 790311; www.museumwales.ac.uk/en/bigpit.

open	All year
tiny campsites' rating	★★★
friendliness	☺ ☺ ☺
cost	BP ££, Couple £££, Family ££££

If ever a hill can be said to cascade down into a valley it's the Blorenge, halfway up which perches the smallholding of Middle Ninfa ('charcoal burner' in Welsh). From its four tiny and secluded wild pitches on the edge of the Brecon Beacons you can imagine yourself an eagle lording it over the Usk Valley

A little closer to hand, though still far below, is the owners' cottage with its tennis-court-cum-croquet-lawn, next to which is a space for another tent or two. Even down here the view is an extraordinary one, off out into the blue and across to the Skirrid mountain.

Around the fire listen out for tawny owls in the woods, the occasional scream of a steam train's whistle and the crack of wood on wood if other guests are playing on the croquet lawn (or the crack of wood on scalp if things have become sufficiently heated). In the morning, expect a visit from a playful cat and two exceedingly gentle horses – a chestnut and a grey – who are all happy to be made a fuss of and are careful not to tread on anything they shouldn't.

A short trek upwards leads to a wonderful nature reserve and pond, while vertigo sufferers can check themselves into a luxurious bunkhouse by the cottage. Meanwhile, the site's eco credentials run to a compost loo in a tiny shed in the garden and a solar-heated shower.

And just in case all this were not heaven enough, you can book yourself a session in Middle Ninfa's very own wood-fired sauna. Just spare everyone the jokes about becoming a Ninfa-maniac.

Pengenffordd
nr Talgarth
Powys
LD3 0EP

Jill Deakin
01874 711353
info@thecastleinn.co.uk
www.thecastleinn.co.uk
OS Landranger: 161 (SO 174 295)

THE BASICS
Size: ⅗ acre.
Pitches: 30 (3 hardstanding).
Terrain: Flat terraces.
Shelter: Yes, all round.
View: Through trees to mountain peaks.
Waterside: No.
Electric hook-ups: 1.
Noise/Light/Olfactory pollution: Some traffic noise from the A479, though this dies down at night.

THE FACILITIES
Loos: 2U **Showers**: 1U (free; hot water; accessible only when the campsite's bunkhouse is occupied).
Other facilities: Washing-up area, picnic tables.
Stuff for children: No.
Recycling: No.

THE RULES
Dogs: Under control.
Fires: No open fires; BBQs off grass.
Other: No parking on grass.

PUB LIFE
The Castle Inn (free house) – log fire, real ales and general cosiness in what was once a farmhouse; open Wed–Fri 6–11.30pm or 'late', Sat 12–'late', Sun till 9pm; food served Wed–Fri 6–9pm, w/es 12–2pm & 6–9pm (Sun till 8pm).
The Mynydd Ddu Tea Rooms in Cwmdu (4 miles; open summer 8am–6pm, winter till 3.30pm 7D; 01874 731077) serve all-day breakfasts, home-cooked meals and prize-winning cakes There are also some pubs in Talgarth (3 miles) for when the Castle Inn is closed.

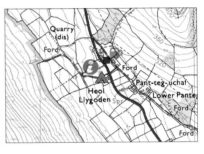

SHOP
Co-op, Talgarth (3 miles) – convenience store with a wide range of goods; open Mon–Fri 7am–10pm, w/es 8am–10pm; 01874 711311.

THERE AND AWAY
Train station: Abergavenny (15 miles) – Newport to Hereford line. The infrequent bus no. X12 (Veolia Transport Cymru) will get you to Talgarth, from where it's a character-building three-mile uphill walk.

OUT AND ABOUT
Welsh Crannog Centre, Llangorse Lake (4½ miles) – a re-creation of a crannog: a house built on an artificial island in a lake or river, as used from prehistoric times all the way up to the Middle Ages; free; open more or less daily in summer 9am–5pm; 01874 658226; see www.llangorselake.co.uk.
Crickhowell (8½ miles) – pleasingly old-fashioned small town in the Usk Valley with very ruined castle (free; always open), tea shops and spectacular bridge over the River Usk; 01873 811970; www.crickhowellinfo.org.uk.

open	All year
tiny campsites' rating	★ ★
friendliness	☺
cost	BP £, Couple ££, Family ££££

High on a pass on the western side of the Black Mountains – specifically between Mynydd Troed and Twyn Mawr – the Castle Inn and its banks of great willowherb are a welcome sight for walkers and cyclists at the end of a long day of heart-quickening climbs and perilous descents. The owners have also taken the trouble of terracing their campsite – top tier for vehicles, bottom two tiers for tents – so there should be no waking up at two o'clock in the morning three metres lower than when you fell asleep.

At the southern end there's a view through trees of Pen Allt-mawr and Pen Gloch-y-pibwr, two peaks that form part of a ridge that makes for an excellent day's circular walk. However, the majority of hikers who stay at this site are here for one thing: an assault on Waun Fach (811 metres), the Black Mountains' highest peak, for which the Castle Inn makes a perfect basecamp. There are two routes up the mountain from here, so summit-baggers can walk up one and down the other. If that seems too energetic, the Iron Age hill-fort-cum-Norman-fortress of Castell Dinas is just behind the inn, and represents a rather softer challenge.

Mountain bikers, meanwhile, come here for the extremely taxing 25-mile Killer Loop (bit.ly/tJfKb1). It starts and ends at the pub, so anyone making it all the way round can either celebrate with a pint or slope off immediately afterwards to die peacefully in their tent.

Should the weather turn particularly waspish or some other such disaster occur, the pub also runs a clean modern bunkhouse and has B&B rooms.

Hay-on-Wye
Hereford
Powys
HR3 5RS

📧 Mrs Zena Davies
☎ 01497 820780
📧 radnorsend@hotmail.com
💻 www.hay-on-wye.co.uk/radnorsend
OS Landranger: 161 (SO 224 431)

THE BASICS
Size: ¾ acre.
Pitches: 15 (0 hardstanding).
Terrain: Flat.
Shelter: On all but the north side.
View: Terrific – over the valley to Hay.
Waterside: No.
Electric hook-ups: 13.
Noise/Light/Olfactory pollution: One lamp to light the way to loos.

THE FACILITIES
Loos: 1M 2W. **Showers**: 1M 1W (20p for '5 min.').
Other facilities: 2 washing-up areas, hot and cold drinks machines, fridge/freezer, 2 seating areas, tumble-dryer (10p for 15 min.), CDP.
Stuff for children: Small adventure playground.
Recycling: Everything.

THE RULES
Dogs: If well behaved and on leads.
Fires: No open fires; BBQs off grass (there are some square stones set in the ground).
Other: No.

PUB LIFE
The Old Black Lion (free house), Hay-on-Wye (¾ mile and a bit tucked away; ask directions when in town) – a 17th-century hotel and posh pub (booking essential); open 8.15am–'late' 7D; food served Mon–Thur 12–2pm & 6.30–9pm, Fri 12–2pm & 6.30–9.30pm, w/es 8.15–9.30am, 12–2.30pm & 6.30–9pm (Sat till 9.30pm); 01497 820841; www.oldblacklion.co.uk.
The Blue Boar (free house), Hay-on-Wye

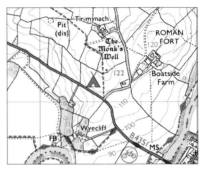

(¾ mile) – more of a pubby pub, is also recommended; 01497 820884.

SHOP
Hay (½ mile) boasts the holy triumvirate of a **Spar**, **Londis** and a **Co-op**, all of which keep long hours.

THERE AND AWAY
Train station: Hereford (21 miles) – Shrewsbury to Newport line. Regular buses travel between Hereford, Hay and Brecon.

OUT AND ABOUT
Hay-on-Wye (½ mile) – 'booktown', with over a million books between the 30-plus bookshops, most of which sell second-hand or antiquarian tomes. There's a helpful 'bookshop map' available at the site. **Paddles and Pedals**, Hay (½ mile) – hire a kayak or Canadian canoe and head off down the River Wye (free pick-up from wherever you finish); £17.50/£25 half/full day per person; open Easter to October; 01497 820604; www.canoehire.co.uk.

open	Early March to end October
tiny campsites' rating	★ ★
friendliness	☺ ☺
cost	BP ££, Couple £££, Family ££££

What nearly everybody does as soon as they've settled in at Radnors End (not so much a campsite as a well-coiffed back garden) is lie back and soak in the views. Ask for a space on the south-eastern side, for there you can enjoy the panorama to the full: seldom since Simon Jones' performances for the 2005 Ashes-winning team has a combination of England and Wales worked so well (and, despite the postal address, the site is in Wales, not

England). There's Herefordshire to the left, Powys to the right – in total a good 180 degrees of wonderful folding hills in every shade of green, with the pretty (sorry, but that is the word for it) town of Hay in the foreground. Mighty Hay Bluff rises above the rooftops like a tricorne hat, with Twmpa (better known as Lord Hereford's Knob) to the south and the Gospel Pass (the route to the ruins of Llanthony Priory) in between.

Loos and showers are in a section of the owners' house, while there are two areas with chairs and tables – one inside a Portakabin (which conveniently also houses a fridge and drinks machines) and one just outside in the garden.

Despite the site's manicured and rather genteel appearance, the clientele tends to the more outdoorsy set, with Wye Valley walkers (www.wyevalleywalk. org), cyclists and canoeists eagerly setting up their little tents and chatting about their day spent in the hills/saddle/water before falling silent to gaze upon the lights of Hay coming on across the valley.

Erwood
Builth Wells
Powys
LD2 3TQ

Nicky and Alistair Legge
01982 560312
mail@trericket.co.uk
www.trericket.co.uk
OS Landranger: 161 (SO 112 413)

THE BASICS
Size: ⅕ acre.
Pitches: 5 (0 hardstanding, though one area is suitable for a vintage VW campervan).
Terrain: Flat.
Shelter: Yes, all round.
View: Up the brook and into the woods, depending on choice of site.
Waterside: The Sgithwen brook runs through the site.
Electric hook-ups: No.
Noise/Light/Olfactory pollution: Traffic on the A470, the gush and flurry of the small river.

THE FACILITIES
Loos: 2U. **Showers**: 1U (free).
Other facilities: Drying room, fridge, campers' shelter with picnic table, bike storage and solar fairy lights; various foodstuffs available for sale. **Stuff for children**: No. **Recycling**: Everything.

THE RULES
Dogs: On leads (ducks and chickens).
Fires: In fire barrels (logs or charcoal £5); BBQs off grass. **Other**: No.

PUB LIFE
Wheelwright Arms (free house), Erwood (1¾ miles) – Victorian pub with restaurant and wood-burning fires; open 11–1am 7D; food served 12–9pm 7D; 01982 560740.

SHOP
Boughrood Stores (2 miles) – village store in a place pronounced 'Bockrood'; open Mon–Fri 8am–1pm & 2–6pm, Sat 8am–1pm, Sun 8.30am–1pm; 01874 754300.

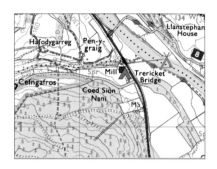

THERE AND AWAY
Train station: Builth Road (11 miles) – Shrewsbury to Swansea line (aka the Heart of Wales line). Bus no. T4 (www.stagecoachbus.com) from Newtown and Merthyr Tydfil via Builth Wells and Brecon will stop at Trericket Mill on request.

OUT AND ABOUT
Erwood Station Craft Centre and Gallery, Erwood (1¾ miles) – craft shop, gallery and tea room with a resident wood-turner on a disused railway station; open daily from St Valentine's Day to Christmas Eve 10am–5.30pm; 01982 560674; www.erwood-station.co.uk.
Wye Valley Walk (100 metres) – a 136-mile walk from Chepstow along the Anglo-Welsh frontier to the source of the Wye at Plynlimon; www.wyevalleywalk.org. The campsite is very well placed for forays to the Victorian spa town of **Builth Wells** (8¼ miles), the riverside bookville that is **Hay-on-Wye** (9¾ miles), and the highly mooch-aroundable market town of **Brecon** (11 miles).

open	Easter to mid October
tiny campsites' rating	★ ★ ★
friendliness	☺ ☺
cost	BP ££, Couple ££££, Family £££££

If a hen creeps up to your picnic table to check if any crumbs have fallen from your pizza, or you find yourself at your tent door watching a parade of ducks crossing a tiny wooden footbridge to graze at the water's edge, there's a good chance you're at Trericket Mill.

The mill in question, on the Sgithwen brook, ground its last corn in the 1930s but has been sympathetically transformed into a B&B with lots of the original machinery still in situ. The mill's back garden, a former cider orchard, is now home to a self-catering cabin (available to rent, from £160/two nights for four people) topped with solar panels and a lovely cosy campsite split into areas of varying sizes, so you can choose to be as private or as sociable during your trip as the mood takes you.

Cross the bridge and walk 100 metres or so upstream through the woods and you can avail yourself of a small plunge pool whose chilly waters are said to be invigorating by all who have survived them. Kayakers and canoeists, meanwhile, can head for the waters of the River Wye, into which the Sgithwen splashes a minute or two after passing the mill.

Avowed non-chefs can order not only a very reasonably priced vegetarian (or vegan) evening meal in the B&B, but breakfast the next morning as well. There's ice cream and pizzas on offer too, as well as pasta, sauces, baked beans and the like for those with a bent to rustle up something for themselves.

Gilfach Farm
Pumsaint
nr Llanwrda
Carmarthenshire
SA19 8YN

Nikki and Oz Omar
01558 650580
nikki@fivesaints.com
www.fivesaints.com
OS Landranger: 146 (SN 663 435)

THE BASICS
Size: ¾ acre.
Pitches: 4 – more if your group hires out the site (0 hardstanding).
Terrain: Slight slope then steeper down to brook.
Shelter: From all sides, depending on where you pitch.
View: Allt Bwlch-y-Gilwen (a hill, your honour).
Waterside: A small brook.
Electric hook-ups: No.
Noise/Light/Olfactory pollution: No.

THE FACILITIES
Loos: 1U in yard & 1U compost loo in field.
Showers: No (adults can take bath in farmhouse for £5).
Other facilities: Washing-up area planned; a lounge for use in wet weather; 8-person tent for hire (£25/week); coarse fishing; dinghy/raft hire for lake (£5/day); horse riding (not pre-bookable) from 30 mins (£10) to 11am–4pm pub or picnic ride (£75); breakfasts and evening meals can be booked in farmhouse; B&B from £35pp.
Stuff for children: A shallow brook. They must be supervised at the lake.
Recycling: Everything.

THE RULES
Dogs: No. **Fires**: Only in brazier (handmade from horseshoes – £5 to hire or £30–£45 to buy) – firewood £5. **Other**: No wandering about in other fields (there are horses). Payment by cash only. Sundry other rules.

PUB LIFE
The Brunant Arms (free house), **Caio** (4 miles) – good food and some hitching

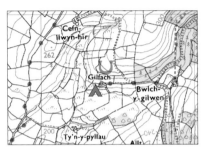

places for horses, if you ride there; open Sun–Thur 11am–11pm, w/es 11am–1am; food served 12–9pm 7D; 01558 650483. The local **Dolaucothi Arms** (Pumsaint) was set to re-open at time of going to print.

SHOP
Free-range eggs, bread rolls and seasonal fruit and veg are available from campsite owners. **Murco**, on the A482 at Crugybar (4 miles) – usual garage-based food and drink; open Mon–Fri 7am–6pm, Sat 8am–4pm, Sun 9am–4pm; 01558 650352.

THERE AND AWAY
Train station: Llanwrda (10½ miles) – Shrewsbury to Swansea line (aka the Heart of Wales line). No onward bus service.

OUT AND ABOUT
Dolaucothi Gold Mines (2 miles) – pan for gold and descend into a Roman mine that was open till the 1930s; adult £7.07, child £3.53, family £17.68 (inc. exhibition and tour); open daily mid March to June & September to October 11am–5pm, July to August 10am–6pm; 01558 650177; NT site.

open	All year
tiny campsites' rating	★ ★
friendliness	☺ ☺ ☺
cost	BP £, Couple ££, Family £££

The roads get narrower and the hills they climb become more ambitious as you approach Gilfach Farm – a sure sign that one's camping experience is not going to be trammelled by the petty irritants of urban life. Indeed, the campsite is even out of sight of the farmhouse and riding stables – there's a field with a lake in it to be crossed before you arrive (the owners will whizz your stuff down on a quad bike if necessary) – leaving the only vestige of civilisation a very tiny but well kept shed that houses the compost loo.

The site's simple treelined field slopes down to a sylvan-topped stream with a view of hilly farmland beyond. If you pop back to the next door field, you can hire a raft or a dinghy for the day and potter about on the small lake with its pair of miniature islands. The countryside around can be explored by bicycle (mountain bikers will love the local forestry tracks), but if you prefer your transport to be more equine-based, horse rides can be arranged with the owners (if the mounts aren't already booked), including a day's jaunt that takes in a pub. Walkers can borrow Fly, the farm's border collie, for a *promenade avec chien*.

Only four tents are allowed at any one time here, but if you happen to hold to Sartre's maxim that 'hell is other people', you can book the whole site and spend your time in wonderful isolation. Breathe in. And out.

60 Ty'n Cornel

Llanddewi Brefi
Tregaron
Ceredigion
SY25 6PH

📧 Richard and Janet Hollins
📞 01980 629259
📧 tyncornel@yha.org.uk
💻 www.elenydd-hostels.co.uk (book
through www.yha.org.uk – where the
spelling is 'Tyncornel')
OS Landranger: 146/147 (SN 751 535)

THE BASICS
Size: ¹⁄₄₀ acre.
Pitches: 5 small (2 hardstanding).
Terrain: Flat.
Shelter: All except to south-west.
View: At head of Doethie Valley.
Waterside: No.
Electric hook-ups: No.
Noise/Light/Olfactory pollution: Only if
someone accidentally leaves the kitchen
light on (in which case you could just turn
it off).

THE FACILITIES
Loos: 1M 1W. **Showers**: 1U (free).
Other facilities: Kitchen (small oven,
gas hobs, microwave, toaster, kettle etc.),
lounge, shelter and bike shed, books,
2 picnic tables.
Stuff for children: Board games and
children's books.
Recycling: Everything (inc. compost).

THE RULES
Dogs: No. **Fires**: No. **Other**: No.

PUB LIFE
The New Inn, Llanddewi Brefi (7¼ miles) –
real ales, open fire and garden with a view
of the Brefi Valley; open Mon 5.30–11pm,
Tue–Fri 11am–4pm & 5.30–11pm, w/es
11am–11pm; food served 12.30–2.30pm
& 5.30–9.30pm 7D (no lunch Mon); 01974
298452; www.newinnllanddewibrefi.co.uk.

SHOP
Siop Brefi, Llanddewi Brefi (7¼ miles) –
convenience store stocking basic supplies;
open Mon–Fri 7am–5.30pm, Sat till 2pm,
Sun 8am–noon; 01974 298240.

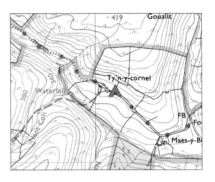

THERE AND AWAY
Train station: The nearest station by
footpath is Cynghordy (10 miles) –
Shrewsbury to Swansea line (aka the
Heart of Wales line). The nearest by road
is Aberystwyth (26 miles). Bus no. 585
(www.arrivabus.co.uk) runs from
Aberystwyth to Llanddewi Brefi, then
it's just a 7-mile walk.

OUT AND ABOUT
Cambrian Way – one guidebook describes
the Doethie Valley as the 'most attractive
valley on the Cambrian Way' and the
long-distance path through it goes right
past the front door of the hostel;
www.cambrianway.org.uk.
Tregaron Red Kite Centre, on the B4343
just outside Tregaron (10 miles) – all the
red kites, local wildlife and info on the
Cors Caron (Tregaron Bog) trails you could
wish for (and a small café too); open daily
Easter to September 10.30am–4.30pm,
October to Easter w/es only 12–4pm;
01974 298977.

CEREDIGION

open	February to November
tiny campsites' rating	★ ★ ★
friendliness	☺ ☺ ☺
cost	BP ££, Couple £££, Family £££££

In a world that would be substantially improved if we all just stayed in bed and thus stopped ourselves from doing bad things, it's heartening to learn of the Elenydd Wilderness Hostels Trust, a group of local people, voluntary wardens and hostellers who got together in 2006 to save the Ty'n Cornel hostel from imminent closure.

The rustic hostel's campsite, also saved for the greater good of humankind, is perfect in its simplicity and sheer tininess. Duck under the washing line and you'll encounter, between a low bank and a thick hawthorn hedge, a narrow strip of grass around which you would not care to swing a cat, even if you were fortunate enough to find one compliant enough to let you. Pop five small tents on here and you'll not have room left over to roast a pickle, as the saying goes in some parts.

Raising the energy to pitch a tent may be the only difficulty you experience. Approaching this former farmstead from the west through Llanddewi Brefi (supposed home of *Little Britain*'s Dafydd, 'the only gay in the village'), the road ascends pitilessly for most of its six miles, until a bumpy and undulating track takes over for the final mile. Arrive from the east and you've a two-mile walk or rough cycle along a track from the nearest road at Soar y Mynydd.

If you arrive in inclement weather, there's a shelter into which you can dive and hang up some wet clothes. But of course this is Wales, so the chances of it raining are pretty slim indeed.

Pentre
Chirk
Denbighshire
LL14 5AW

Gail and Richard Lewis
01978 823184 & 07773 209403
OS Landranger: 117 (SJ 291 412)

THE BASICS
Size: ⅔ acre.
Pitches: Variable (6 hardstanding).
Terrain: Flat.
Shelter: Mature wood on western side.
View: The A438 bridge, off to the east.
Waterside: No.
Electric hook-ups: 12
Noise/Light/Olfactory pollution: Some traffic noise and street lights.

THE FACILITIES
Loos (portaloo): 1U. **Showers**: No (but pending).
Other facilities: Free-range eggs for sale.
Stuff for children: No.
Recycling: Everything.

THE RULES
Dogs: Under control; ask for permission before taking dogs onto farmland.
Fires: No open fires; BBQs off grass.
Other: No.

PUB LIFE
The Telford Inn (free house), Trevor (1¾ miles) – a picture-perfect pub at the northern end of the Pontcysyllte Aqueduct; open April to October 11am–11pm 7D, otherwise Mon–Fri 11am–3pm & 6–11pm, w/es 11am–11pm; food served 11am–9pm 7D April to October, 11am–2.30pm & 6–9pm at other times; 01978 820469.

SHOP
Co-op, Chirk (2 miles) – mini supermarket; open Mon–Fri 5.30am (yes!)–10pm, Sat 7am–10pm, Sun 8am–10pm; 01691 772979.

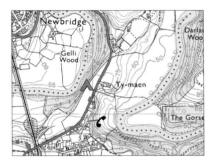

THERE AND AWAY
Train station: Ruabon (3 miles) – Shrewsbury to Chester line. Bus no. 2/2A (www.arrivabus.co.uk) run frequently from Ruabon to Pentre.

OUT AND ABOUT
Pontcysyllte Aqueduct (1½ miles) – Thomas Telford and William Jessop's 1805 masterpiece on the Llangollen branch of the Shropshire Union Canal; free; always open; chirk.com/aqueduct.html.
Chirk Castle, Chirk (3 miles) – an extremely impressive 700-year-old fortress built by Roger Mortimer for Edward I; adult £9, child £4.50, family £22.50; open March to June Wed–Sun, July to October daily 10am–5pm; some other days during rest of year; 01691 777701; NT site.
AngloWelsh Boats, Trevor (1¾ miles) – chug along the Llangollen Canal for a day; day boat hire from £99 for up to 10 people; 01173 041122; www.anglowelsh.co.uk.

open	All year
tiny campsites' rating	★
friendliness	☺ ☺ ☺
cost	BP ££, Couple ££, Family ££

Any initial disappointment at discovering that the slim strip of field given over to camping is severed from the farm itself by a road is tempered by the knowledge that here at Ty Maen you are not only in the hands of wonderfully friendly hosts, but you are also perfectly positioned for assaults on a veritable cornucopia of eclectic attractions.

The facilities here are undeniably basic: some recycling bins and a one-person portaloo (albeit a posh and immaculately clean one) are more or less it, though there are plans afoot to add a shower. Meanwhile, bat-lovers will be very happy to learn that some of the trees along the western edge of the field play host to boxes frequented by pipistrelles.

Across the road, Ty Maen ('Stone House') farm is populated by cows, sheep and pigs. There are no public footpaths through the farm but, on request, owners Gail and Richard will allow campers through the fields down to the River Dee, which all but encircles their land in a big lazy loop. They will also ferry car-less campers down to the pub and back of an evening, if given a bit of advance warning.

Nearby there's the Offa's Dyke path, the Shropshire Union Canal (and its frankly unmissable aqueduct at Pontcysyllte), Chirk Castle, the Llangollen steam railway (www.llangollen-railway.co.uk) and the romantic ruins of Dinas Brân (www.castlewales.com/dinas.html). However, hang around at the site in the evening and you'll find the lights of the distant traffic on the A483 bridge make for a sight that is curiously compelling. Who says there is no mystery in modern life?

Ty Newydd Isaf
Betws Gwerfil Goch
Corwen
Denbighshire
LL21 9PT

Richard Wootton
☎ 07927 775395
✉ richard.t.wootton@gmail.com
🖥 buzzardrockcampingclub.co.uk
OS Landranger: 116 (SJ 033 465)

THE BASICS
Size: 1/13 acre.
Pitches: 7 (0 hardstanding).
Terrain: Sloping – some pitches very slopey.
Shelter: From all sides but north.
View: Llantysilio and Brenig mountain ranges.
Waterside: No.
Electric hook-ups: No.
Noise/Light/Olfactory pollution: Nothing but the lights from the village below, the sounds of the river in the valley and the hoots of the tawny owls.

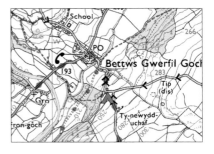

THE FACILITIES
Loos: 1U. **Showers**: 1U (free); 1U hydrobath (small charge).
Other facilities: No. **Stuff for children**: No.
Recycling: Everything (inc. compost).

THE RULES
Dogs: Under control. **Fires**: Each pitch has its own firepit. **Other**: Large groups at owner's discretion.

PUB LIFE
The Goat Inn (free house), Maerdy (2 miles) – 17th-century coaching inn serving home-cooked food; open Mon–Fri 5.30pm–midnight, Sat 4.30pm–midnight, Sun noon–midnight; food served Fri–Sat 6–9pm, Sun 12–7.30pm; 01490 460536. Corwen (4 miles) has a number of pubs serving food during the week.

SHOP
Rhug Estate Farm Shop (2miles), on the A5 between Corwen and Maerdy – a huge sweep of produce, much of which is locally produced and/or organic, with a restaurant

too; Mon–Thur 8am–5.30pm; Fri–Sat 8am–6pm, Sun 8.30am–6pm; 01490 413000; rhug.co.uk. Corwen has a plethora of little shops.

THERE AND AWAY
Train station: Both Ruabon to the east and Betws-y-Coed to the west are about 20 miles away. From Ruabon, take bus no. 5 to Llangollen (www.bryn-melyn.co.uk) then no. 91 to Betws Gwerfil Goch (www.ghacoaches.co.uk).

OUT AND ABOUT
Brenig Way (bit.ly/pQ7B76) – the 32-mile walking route runs from Corwen to Llyn Brenig (5½ miles; bit.ly/pOZvAJ) and passes through a neighbouring field. Try the mountain bike trails in **Clocaenog Forest** (5 miles) ranging from 20 to 35 miles; www.ridehiraethog.com; or the family-friendly **Brenig Trail**, a 9½-mile cycle path starting and finishing at Llyn Brenig. Meanwhile, the **Llangollen Railway** steams along the Dee Valley from Llangollen to Carrog (6¼ miles); 01978 860979; www.llangollen-railway.co.uk.

open	All year
tiny campsites' rating	★ ★
friendliness	☺ ☺ ☺
cost	BP £, Couple ££, Family ££

This is not a site that spends its cash on looking flash and grabbing your attention, but rather revels in giving guests an experience as close to wild camping as it's possible to have. Sliding down the rugged hill that rises steeply from the little village of Betws Gwerfil Goch, the newly created site comprises a mere half-dozen pitches, most of which accommodate but a single tent. There are two high pitches offering the best mountain views; a brace of lower, more sheltered pitches; and a couple at the foot of the field 'for when it gets a bit blowy'. Each and every one of them is a proud owner of a firepit and campfires are actively encouraged.

In the spring and summer the field turns into a meadow, its seemingly vertical nature giving it an alpine appearance (only slightly diluted by the telegraph poles that stride across it). But what makes the Buzzard Rock Camping Club unique is the range of optional extra-tentular activities that the resourceful owner Richard lays on. From guided walks to martial arts lessons via bushcraft, relaxation therapy, meditation, bat walks, fly fishing and pond dipping, there's something to froth everyone's coffee, and prices begin at the excessively reasonable £5/hour per group.

Come the evening, you can practise those new found relaxation therapy skills in the hydrobath – certainly not something you'll be able to do every time you go on a wild camping trip.

Carmel
Llanrwst
Conwy
LL26 0NT

Mr and Mrs G Griffiths
01492 640730
maesybryncampsite@hotmail.co.uk
www.maesybryncampsite.co.uk
Landranger: 116 (SH 836 637)

THE BASICS
Size: 1 acre.
Pitches: 30 (1 hardstanding).
Terrain: Mainly flat.
Shelter: Most sides.
View: Denbigh Moors.
Waterside: At the foot of the site runs a stream called the Cyll.
Electric hook-ups: 10.
Noise/Light/Olfactory pollution: A light shines out from the loo.

THE FACILITIES
Loos: 3M (plus urinals) 3W. **Showers**: 2M 2W (free).
Other facilities: Washing machine (£1), tumble-dryer (£1), washing-up sinks, a few basics for sale (long-life milk, cereal, soup, home laid free-range eggs, toothpaste etc.), CDP. **Stuff for children**: Playing in the stream, feeding the chickens, befriending the cats. **Recycling**: Everything.

THE RULES
Dogs: On leads; owners must fill in a form accepting care and responsibility for their pets. **Fires**: No open fires; a supply of bricks for BBQs off grass.
Other: No cars between 11pm and 7am.

PUB LIFE
The Old Stag (free house), Llangernyw (3¾ miles) – real ales and an award-winning menu in a farmhouse beside a 4,500-year-old yew; open Mon 5.30–10.30pm, Tue–Thur 12–3pm & 5.30–10.30pm, Fri–Sat 12–3pm & 5.30pm–midnight, Sun 12–10.30pm; food served Mon 5.30–8.30pm, Tue–Sat 12–2.30pm & 5.30–8.30pm, Sun 12–8.30pm; 01745 860213; www.theoldstag.com.

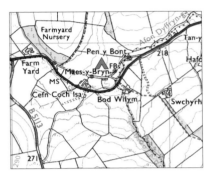

SHOP
Spar, Llanrwst (3¼ miles) – large convenience store; 6.30am–11pm 7D; 01492 640428. There's also a wide variety of shops in Llanrwst (though few open on Sundays, this being God-fearing country).

THERE AND AWAY
Train station: Llanrwst (3 miles) – Llandudno Junction to Blaenau Ffestiniog line (aka the Conwy Valley line). Take a taxi from there on in (see opposite).

OUT AND ABOUT
Tree Top Adventure, Trefriw (6 miles) – high-level treetop thrills with zip lines and something called a POWERFAN™; (from) adult £25, U16 £20, family £80; 01690 710914; www.ttadventure.co.uk. **Swallow Falls**, nr Betws-y-Coed (8 miles) – a series of charming waterfalls along the River Llugwy; adult £1.50, child 50p, open all year 24 hours a day; 01690 710770; bit.ly/rqa4WW.

open	Easter to October
tiny campsites' rating	★ ★
friendliness	☺ ☺ ☺
cost	BP ££, Couple £££, Family ££££

Welsh names, eh? They sound all mystical and dreamlike, but translate them into English and what happens? Ty Mawr becomes 'Big House', Hafod Uchaf is reduced to 'Upper Farm', while Gwersyll Maes-y-Bryn subsides into the disappointingly prosaic 'Field on the Hill Campsite'. Perhaps we'd enjoy life more if we ditched English, which no one wants to learn anyway, and conversed in the tongue of Dafydd ap Gwilym and Taliesin.

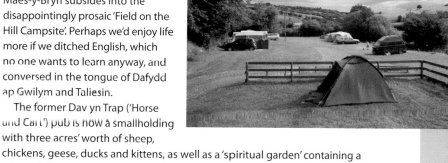

The former Dav yn Trap ('Horse and Cart') pub is now a smallholding with three acres' worth of sheep, chickens, geese, ducks and kittens, as well as a 'spiritual garden' containing a labyrinth – not something you get at every campsite. The very friendly Welsh-speaking owners really make their guests feel at home, while the site itself is on two levels, the lower one tending to be more sociable, and the upper terrace appealing to slightly less touchy-feely types. There's also a miniature field to one side that is home to a yurt (bookable from Easter to October).

Perched on a range of hills opposite Snowdonia, three miles up from the small town of Llanrwst, this location rewards campers with a fine view of Mynydd Hiraethog (the Denbigh Moors) to the north.

Llanrwst is worth a visit for its bridge, almshouse museum and plucky if slightly delusional sense of its own independence. The small town possesses a coat of arms and a flag, and glories in the motto Cymru, Lloegr a Llanrwst ('Wales, England and Llanrwst'). Local taxi firm Parker's Private Hire (01492 641010) will transport you from the campsite to this small Snowdonian republic for £6.

Cynefin
Betws Garmon
nr Caernarfon
Gwynedd
LL54 7YR

Ian and Marion Macleod
01286 650707
camping@silver-birches.org.uk
www.silver-birches.org.uk
Landranger: 115 (SH 544 567)

THE BASICS

Size: ¾ acre.
Pitches: 13 (1 hardstanding).
Terrain: Mainly flat.
Shelter: Yes, though some wind from south.
View: Mynydd Mawr.
Waterside: A nameless stream near pitches 8 & 9.
Electric hook-ups: 3.
Noise/Light/Olfactory pollution: The fast-flowing stream chits and chats its way over the stones.

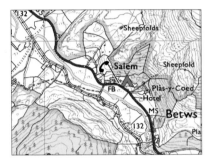

THE FACILITIES

Loos: 3U. **Showers**: 2U (free).
Other facilities: 2 washrooms, 2 washing-up areas, washing machine, tumble-dryer, freezer, microwave, book swap, info leaflet area, picnic tables, hairdryer and free wi-fi.
Stuff for children: No.
Recycling: Everything.

THE RULES

Dogs: On leads and by prior arrangement only.
Fires: No open fires; BBQs off grass.
Other: No children under 15. Cars off grass.

PUB LIFE

The closest pub is in Waunfawr (2 miles), but a much better option is the **Cwellyn Arms** (free house), Rhyd Ddu (3¼ miles) – a roadside inn with a log fire and real ale; open from 10am 7D, closing time depends on season (roughly between 9pm & midnight); food served 11am–9pm 7D (breakfast from 8am can be booked the day before); 01766 890321; www.snowdoninn.co.uk.

SHOP

Waunfawr Village Shop (2¼ miles) – store with wee off licence; Mon–Fri 7.30am–6pm, Sat 8am–5.30pm, Sun 8.30am–12.30pm; 01286 650834. The **Village Chippy** opens lunchtime Sat and 5.30–9pm (to 10pm if busy) Tue–Sat; 01286 650683.

THERE AND AWAY

Train station: Bangor (14 miles) – Crewe to Holyhead line (aka the North Wales Coast line). From Bangor, take bus no. 10 to Caernarfon from where the S4 to Beddgelert stops at the site.

OUT AND ABOUT

Beddgelert (7 miles) – charming village on the River Glaslyn that's well worth a snoop around; www.beddgelerttourism.com. **Welsh Highland Railway** (nearest station Plas y Nant; ½ mile) – the world's most powerful 2-foot-long steam trains whizz through Snowdonia; return fare Caernarfon to Porthmadog: adult £32, (see website for kids); almost daily service April to October; www.welshhighlandrailway.net.

open	March to October
tiny campsites' rating	★ ★
friendliness	☺ ☺ ☺
cost	BP ££, Couple £££, Family ££££

Silver Birches is definitely a site for grown-ups. There's the book swap, the well-ordered pitches marked with bookees' names and the very civilised and wide-ranging facilities, but the clincher is the fact that children under 15 are barred from entry. Thus, it's no surprise that this site is very popular with teachers and others who, while they love children dearly, are very happy to be without their company every once in a while.

The lowering presence here is of the mountain opposite which, despite being a mere five miles from Snowdon, the Welsh still call Mynydd Mawr ('Big Mountain'). Behind, out of sight, is Moel Eilio, which is no shrinking violet either. The two serve as a palate-whetting hors d'oeuvre to Snowdon itself. The Snowdon Ranger path – one of the less-populated routes up Wales' highest mountain – is less than two miles from the campsite and, frankly, it would be rude not to take advantage of the fact, especially now that the £8.4-million summit café is open.

A regular bus service stops just outside the site linking it with Caernarfon (whose castle is well worth a visit), the Snowdon Ranger path and Beddgelert.

Campsite owners Ian and Marion have thoughtfully produced a book of ideas for things to do in the local area that includes walks illustrated so well with their own photographs that they make getting lost the sole preserve of the preternaturally disorientated.

Treheli
Rhiw
Pwllheli
Gwynedd
LL53 8AA

Mr Williams
01758 780281
OS Landranger: 123 (SH 239 285)

THE BASICS
Size: 6/7 acre.
Pitches: Variable (0 hardstanding).
Terrain: Flat.
Shelter: Some on the north side, but very exposed to sea winds.
View: The whole of Porth Niegwl ('Hell's Mouth Bay').
Waterside: A 3-minute walk to the sea.
Electric hook-ups: No.
Noise/Light/Olfactory pollution: The long withdrawing roar of the waves below.

THE FACILITIES
Loos: 5U. **Showers:** 2U (20p for '5 min.').
Other facilities: No.
Stuff for children: Swings on trees.
Recycling: No.

THE RULES
Dogs: On leads. **Fires:** No open fires; BBQs allowed. **Other:** No.

PUB LIFE
The Sun Inn (Robinson's), Llanengan (5¾ miles) – friendly country pub with beer garden; open summer 11am–11pm 7D, winter Mon–Fri 12–3pm & 5–11pm, w/es 12–11pm; food served 12–2pm & 6–9pm 7D; 01758 712660; www.thesuninnllanengan.co.uk.

SHOP
Ty Siop Llangian, Llangian (4¼ miles) – minimal stock; open Mon–Tue & Thur–Fri 7.30am–noon & 1–5pm; Wed & w/es 7.30am–noon; 01758 712095. There is also a small store at Aberdaron (5 miles) and a variety of shops at the attractive resort town of Abersoch (6 miles).

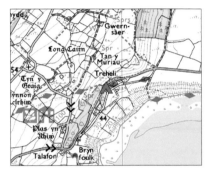

THERE AND AWAY
Train station: Pwllheli (10 miles) – Pwllheli to Shrewsbury line. Bus no. 17B (Nefyn Coaches) from Pwllheli stops down the lane from the site.

OUT AND ABOUT
Plas yn Rhiw (¼ mile) – a splendid little manor house with a fine ornamental garden; adult £4, child £2, family £10; open April to September Thur–Sun 12–5pm (plus some Mon & Wed), October Thur–Sun 12–4pm; 01758 780219; NT site. The beach at **Porth Ysgo** (3½ miles) is renowned among the climbing set for its curious but highly scalable gabbro boulders; bit.ly/rr7NCp.

open	Easter to October
tiny campsites' rating	★ ★
friendliness	☺
cost	BP £££, Couple £££, Family £££

Arguably the ultimate expression of the tiny campsite: not only is Treheli already admirably compact, but it's actually getting smaller every year. Perched above Hell's Mouth Bay, the cliffs beneath it are so friable that over the years its three tiers have been reduced to one, and the time is coming when that too will have crumbled away and the campsite will disappear.

So, there's no time to waste if you wish to sample the uninterrupted sea views; the precipitous three-minute walk down to the sandy beach; the sheep being driven right through the site of an evening; the chance visits from pheasants; the determinedly rustic facilities (mystifyingly there's no loo roll provided, so remember to take your own) and the informal cliff-top camping experience. The total lack of signage to – and even at – the farm means that you'll be advised to take a map along too.

The locals acknowledge that there is something of a dearth of good pubs in the vicinity (and a complete absence of them close by) until you reach the Sun Inn at Llanengan. It's nearly six miles by road, but if you walk there via the beach (making sure to avoid high tide) it cuts it down to about four, and makes for a bracing pre-prandial stroll.

Sadly, the rigidly enforced flat fee per group, regardless of size, puts Treheli in the running for the title of 'Britain's Most Expensive Site for the Solo Camper'. On the upside, if you were to pack a couple of enormo-tents and take along everyone you know, you could enjoy the cheapest holiday imaginable.

Scotland

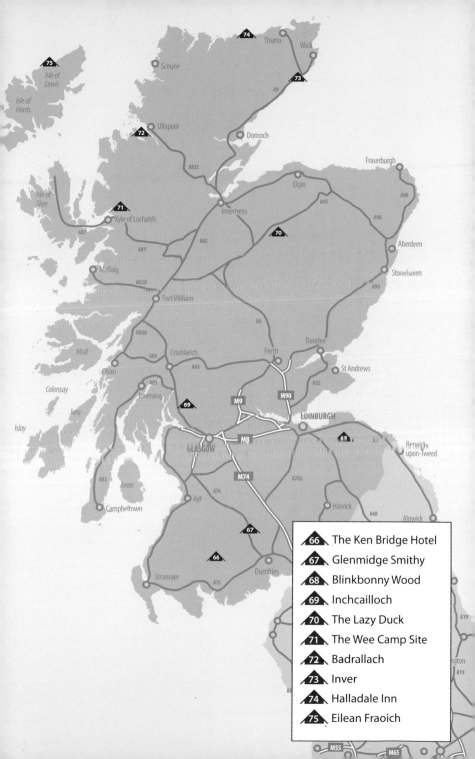

66	The Ken Bridge Hotel
67	Glenmidge Smithy
68	Blinkbonny Wood
69	Inchcailloch
70	The Lazy Duck
71	The Wee Camp Site
72	Badrallach
73	Inver
74	Halladale Inn
75	Eilean Fraoich

New Galloway
Dumfries and Galloway
DG7 3PR

@ Dave and Sue Paterson
☎ 01644 420211
✍ mail@kenbridgehotel.co.uk
💻 www. kenbridgehotel.co.uk
OS Landranger: 83 (NX 641 783)

THE BASICS
Size: ½ acre.
Pitches: Variable; 'we don't like to overcrowd it' (0 hardstanding).
Terrain: Mainly flat.
Shelter: Yes.
View: Ken Bridge.
Waterside: Yes, the Water of Ken.
Electric hook-ups: 5.
Noise/Light/Olfactory pollution: No.

THE FACILITIES
Loos: 2U. **Showers**: 1U (free).
Other facilities: CDP.
Stuff for children: No.
Recycling: Bottles, cans, paper.

THE RULES
Dogs: No dogs.
Fires: No open fires; BBQs well off grass.
Other: No.

PUB LIFE
The Ken Bridge Hotel (free house) – in the CAMRA *Good Beer Guide* and boasting a wide selection of malt whisky, the bar is open throughout the day in summer for cream teas and snacks including soup, chips and sandwiches; open 11am–midnight 7D; meals served 12–2pm & 5.30–8.30pm 7D.

SHOP
JR Hopkins, New Galloway (1 mile) – basics plus some fruit & veg; open Mon–Fri 7.30am–5.30pm, Sat 8am–5pm, Sun 8.30am–1pm; 01644 420229. There is also a small shop up the hill in Balmaclellan (1 mile) – closed Sun – and a clog and shoe workshop.

THERE AND AWAY
Train station: Dumfries (24 miles) – Glasgow Central to Carlisle line. From Dumfries take bus no. 500 to Castle Douglas then no. S2 or 520 to the site.

OUT AND ABOUT
Southern Upland Way – Scotland's 212-mile coast-to-coast trail passes close by at the wonderfully named St John's Town of Dalry (2½ miles); www. southernuplandway.gov.uk. The hotel can organise lifts and baggage transfers.
Loch Ken (4 miles) – sailing, windsurfing, kayaking, canoeing, climbing, archery and (of course) an outdoor laser quest; 01644 420626; www.lochken.co.uk.
Seven Stanes (various distances) – 5 of the 7 Stanes, which offer some of the best mountain bike trails in Britain, are within striking distance of the site; 01387 272440; www.7stanes.gov.uk.

open	All year (depending on river)
tiny campsites' rating	★ ★ ★
friendliness	☺ ☺ ☺
cost	BP ££, Couple £££, Family £££

Deep in the heart of Dumfries and Galloway runs the wondrously named Water of Ken. At the elegant Ken Bridge, just 10 miles from the river's source, it already demands five full spans to cross it, having by then incorporated the Rivers Dee, Doon and Deugh. Beside the Ken Bridge stands an 18th-century coaching inn whose lovely diminutive beer garden extends, apparently unwittingly, into a small riverside field. This, it turns out, is the campsite, and the combination of river, welcoming pub and surrounding hills makes it a little cracker.

Otters patrol the river, and if you wish to compete with them for food, including the invasive crayfish, the fishing is free for campers. Bird-lovers, meanwhile, can look out for kingfishers and ospreys on the Ken or follow the nearby Galloway Kite Trail, a circular route that takes in the best places to see these magnificent birds of prey, which have been successfully reintroduced to the area.

New Galloway (the smallest royal borough in Scotland, fact fans) is only a mile away and, though just a wee village, it boasts a highly regarded arts performance space called CatStrand (www.catstrand.com) whose varied programme is always worth checking.

Further afield, Castle Douglas is Scotland's Food Town (13 miles; www.cd-foodtown.org), Kirkcudbright (18 miles; www.kirkcudbright.co.uk), its Artists' Town and Wigtown (25 miles) its Book Town. The last fair bursts at the seams with bookshops – second-hand and new – and there's an annual 10-day literary festival in September (www.wigtownbookfestival.com).

· Glenmidge
Auldgirth
Dumfries and Galloway
DG2 0SW

James (aka Hamish) and Margaret Steele

01387 740328

OS Landranger: 78 (NX 891 870)

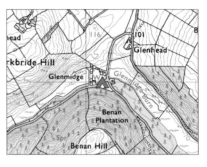

THE BASICS
Size: ½ acre.
Pitches: Variable (3 hardstanding).
Terrain: Flat.
Shelter: Yes.
View: Hills.
Waterside: A nameless burn runs by.
Electric hook-ups: 16.
Noise/Light/Olfactory pollution: No.

THE FACILITIES
Loos: 1U. **Showers**: 1U (free).
Other facilities: Washing-up area, electric
hob, microwave, kettle, toaster, table and
chairs, fridge, tourist information, washing
machine, CDP, owners' honey for sale.
Stuff for children: No.
Recycling: Everything.

THE RULES
Dogs: On leads (there's a doggy run
around the corner).
Fires: No open fires; BBQs off grass
(bricks may be borrowed).
Other: Adults only (16+) on site.

PUB LIFE
Auldgirth Inn (free house; 2 miles) – a
friendly pub on the edge of the village;
open Mon–Tue 5pm–midnight, Wed–Fri
12–2.30pm & 5pm–midnight, w/es
noon–midnight; food served Mon–Tue
5.30–8.30pm, Wed–Fri 12–2pm &
5.30–8.30pm, Sat 12–8.30pm, Sun till 8pm;
01387 740250; www.auldgirthinn.co.uk.

SHOP
Auldgirth Stores (1¾ miles) – basics plus
some fruit & veg, with tea room attached;
shop open Mon–Sat 7.30am–6pm, Sun

9am–4pm (till noon in winter); tea room
open summer Mon–Sat 7.30am–5pm, Sun
11am–4pm, winter Mon–Sat 7.30am-4pm;
01387 740235.

THERE AND AWAY
Train station: Dumfries (8 miles) –
Glasgow to Carlisle line. Bus no. 246 from
Dumfries (www.stagecoachbus.com) stops
at Auldgirth, 2 miles from Glenmidge.

OUT AND ABOUT
Drumlanrig Castle (9 miles) – a late-
17th-century castle in the Renaissance
style, country estate, cycle museum,
gardens and home to the Buccleuch
art collection; adult £9, child (3–16) £5,
family £26; castle open daily April to
August 11am–4pm; 01848 331555;
www.drumlanrig.com.
Seven Stanes (various distances; see The
Ken Bridge Hotel entry, p166). Hire bikes
from Rik's Bike Shed and Cycle Museum at
Drumlanrig Castle; 01848 330080.

open	March to November
tiny campsites' rating	★ ★
friendliness	☺ ☺
cost	BP £, Couple ££, Family £££

The hamlet of Glenmidge, 11 miles north of Dumfries, is hidden in a complex network of narrow roads spread around farms that sprawl over low tumbling hills. The former blacksmith's house in the settlement now hosts a small, well-sheltered campsite with a view over the hedge to some of those hills and access to more prime cycling country than is either good or proper.

A building that might be either a small barn or a large shed has been kitted out with every mod con, including a dining area – a boon for those one or two days a year when Scotland experiences rain. The barn/ shed also contains handy maps of the local area for those wanting to walk or cycle. At night, though, you can just lie back and watch the stars come out to twinkle; laminated charts are available to help you sort your Ursa Major from your Andromeda.

Happily, Glenmidge does not owe its name to the small biting insect for which Scotland is rightly famous, but is derived from the Gaelic

for 'small glen'. Like the rest of Scotland (and, lest we forget, parts of the far north of England), the site is susceptible to the odd midge in summer, but only on days when there is no wind (see Top Tips, p13, for midge-repelling strategies).

This quiet site is for adults only, though as children are assumed to have morphed into adults by the time they are 16, this means that parents can take along any older teenagers who still deign to holiday with them.

nr Longyester
East Lothian
EH41 4PL (don't use for
satnav – see website
for directions)

📧 Steven and Sally Wray
📞 01620 825034 & 07976 871885
📧 s.wray999@btinternet.com
🖥 www.blinkbonnywood.com
OS Landranger: 66 (NT 542 643)

THE BASICS
Size: ⅛ acre.
Pitches: 4 (0 hardstanding).
Terrain: Can be a bit boggy if wet, flat/sloping depending on pitch.
Shelter: Yes, for both woodland pitches; other 2 sheltered by woods behind and low bracken to north.
View: From the 2 woodside pitches glorious vista towards Firth of Forth.
Waterside: No.
Electric hook-ups: No.
Noise/Light/Olfactory pollution: Just the enchanting sounds of the forest.

THE FACILITIES
Loos (compost): 1U. **Showers**: No.
Other facilities: Handmade wooden objects for sale.
Stuff for children: No.
Recycling: Glass, paper, card.

THE RULES
Dogs: Kept on a lead. **Fires**: Firepit for each pitch. A small amount of firewood is provided – additional supplies £2.50/bag.
Other: No.

PUB LIFE
The Goblin Ha' (free house), Gifford (3 miles) – open fires, real ales and a wide range of food; bar open Mon–Thur 4–11pm, Fri–Sat 11am–1am, Sun 11am–11pm; food served 8–11am & 12–9.30pm; 01620 810244; www.goblinha.com.

SHOP
Co-op, Gifford (3 miles) – small supermarket; open Mon–Sat 7am–10pm, Sun 8am–10pm; 01620 810216.

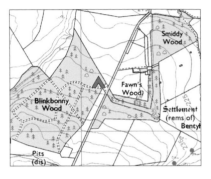

THERE AND AWAY
Train station: Longniddry or Drem (both 13 miles) – North Berwick to Edinburgh line. From Longniddry take bus no. 128 (Eve Coaches; 01368 865500) to Haddington then no. 123 (www.firstgroup.com) to Gifford, 3 miles from Blinkbonny.

OUT AND ABOUT
There are 5 signposted footpaths (bit.ly/pcd3tV) across the **Lammermuir Hills**, one of which (no.1) runs from Gifford to Carfraemill via Blinkbonny. Meanwhile, the most northerly section of the 212-mile **Southern Upland Way** (www.southernuplandway.gov.uk) can be joined at Longformacus (13 miles). Otherwise, you could visit the **Pishwanton Project** – not, as the name suggests, a top secret mission to communicate with alien beings, but a Life Science Trust centre whose aim is to 'rediscover a healing, physical and spiritual connection with the natural world'; 01620 810259; pishwanton.org.

open	April to October
tiny campsites' rating	★ ★
friendliness	☺ ☺ ☺
cost	BP ££, Couple ££, Family £££

When the directions to a campsite start to rely on ever more insignificant centres of population as landmarks along the way, and end with a plangent plea not to use a satnav, you can be fairly sure that something pleasingly out of the way awaits you.

Such is the case with Blinkbonny Wood. Blink bonnily or otherwise and you'll miss the tiny sign to your right inviting you up a rutted track and into its 100 acres of Japanese larch, Scots pine and Norway spruce. There are just four pitches – two on the edge of the wood with soul-easing views out to the Firth of Forth (15 or so miles away) and, for lovers of solitude, a pair in separate glades within.

Mild camping this is not. There's a proudly rustic compost toilet, firepits at each pitch and some logs to sit on, but no shower or standpipe. Clean water for washing and cooking comes in large plastic containers and, if you're finickity about your drinking water, you can purchase a bottle or two from the owners.

Should you ever tire of reconnoitring the woods or hugging the trees, you need simply to turn right out of the exit and you're climbing the shamefully under-explored Lammermuir Hills. Come later on in the season if you wish to see them turn purple under heather, amid which black grouse and ptarmigan lurk, harming no one.

And, at the end of your stay, you can pick up a memento – bird boxes, flower presses and benches handmade by the owner from Blinkbonny's own trees.

Port Bawn
Inchcailloch
nr Balmaha
Stirlingshire

Charlie Croft
01389 722600
inchcailloch@lochlomond-trossachs.org
bit.ly/oL0Zzx
OS Landranger: 56 (NS 407 901)

THE BASICS
Size: ¼ acre.
Pitches: 12 people max. on site
(0 hardstanding).
Terrain: Flat grass beneath trees.
Shelter: Yes, from all sides.
View: Loch Lomond & mountains behind.
Waterside: Yes.
Electric hook-ups: No.
Noise/Light/Olfactory pollution: No.

THE FACILITIES
Loos (compost): 1U. **Showers**: No.
Other facilities: 6 large picnic tables.
Stuff for children: No.
Recycling: Take all rubbish and recycling
with you.

THE RULES
Dogs: Under strict control.
Fires: 2 half oil-drums for fires on beach;
BBQ platform on each picnic table.
Other: Max. stay 2 nights. Don't disturb
wildlife. NB There are no standpipes on the
island so bring your own water or some
means of making the loch water potable.

PUB LIFE
Oak Tree Inn (free house), Balmaha
(10-minute ferry ride) – former 'Gastro
Pub of the Year' and priding itself in its
malt whiskies, locally brewed ales and
traditional Scottish cooking; open
8am–'late' 7D; food served 12–9pm 7D;
01360 870357, www.oak-tree-inn.co.uk.

SHOP
Right next door to the Oak Tree Inn is the
Village Shop, which stocks the basics and
a few more-exotic items and gifts (there's

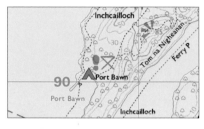

an ATM here too, though not a free one);
open Mon–Sat 7.30am–10pm, Sun 8am–
10pm; 01360 870270.

THERE AND AWAY
Train station: Balloch Central (12 miles
and ferry ride) – Glasgow Queen Street
to Balloch Central line. Then bus no. 309
to Balmaha. Ferry to Inchcailloch from
MacFarlane's Boatyard, Balmaha (adult £5
return, child (U14) £2.50; 01360 870214;
www.balmahaboatyard.co.uk – no
timetable: ferry runs on request. Foot
passengers only.

OUT AND ABOUT
Loch Lomond and the Trossachs – 720
square miles of wonderment in which
to walk, cycle, ride, watch wildlife, canoe,
sail or waterski; 01389 722600;
www.lochlomond-trossachs.org.
Hire a boat at **MacFarlane's Boatyard**,
Balmaha (where you catch the ferry); open
summer 9am–8pm, non-summer 9am–
5pm, no hires after 5pm; clinker-built boats
with motor £20/hour, £50/day; without
motor (but with oars) £10/hour, £30/day;
01360 870214; balmahaboatyard.co.uk.
Various afternoon cruises also available.

open	All year
tiny campsites' rating	★ ★ ★
friendliness	☺ ☺
cost	BP £, Couple ££, Family £££

Step off the tiny ferry onto Inchcailloch, the largest of a string of islands at the southern end of Loch Lomond, and you and your camping gear enter the world of the MacGregors. The world of deceased MacGregors, more correctly, because the lawless clan used it as their burial ground for many centuries – and had need to, given their continual run-ins with the even less law-abiding MacFarlanes (who made so many nocturnal raids on cattle that the moon became known as 'MacFarlane's Lantern'). The MacGregors are, however, comparatively modern interlopers. Meaning 'island of the old women' in English, Inchcailloch (sometimes called Inchcailleach) is reputed to have been the site of a nunnery in ages past. The fair St Kentigerna lived here, and indeed took it upon herself to die here back in 733. The ruins of a 13th-century church bearing her name can still be seen on the island.

Blissfully, there are no roads on the 130-acre isle, but merely a number of well signposted footpaths. From the jetty, one such takes travellers two-thirds of a mile through a wooded valley to Port Bawn, a natural harbour and home to a small lochside clearing that serves as a campsite. Come night-time, you, your fellow campers (only a dozen are allowed) and the birds (redstarts, woodpeckers, treecreepers and more) have this achingly beautiful nature reserve to yourselves.

The only other residents are fallow deer, elusive descendents of those brought here by King Robert the Bruce (so if at first you don't see one, try try try again).

Nethy Bridge
Inverness-shire
PH25 3ED

David and Valery Dean
lazyduckhostel@gmail.com
www.lazyduck.co.uk
OS Landranger: 36 (NJ 016 204)

THE BASICS
Size: ⅕ acre.
Pitches: 4 (0 hardstanding).
Terrain: Slightly undulating.
Shelter: Yes.
View: Field with Soay sheep, lazy Aylesbury ducks and hens.
Waterside: Burn and ponds.
Electric hook-ups: No.
Noise/Light/Olfactory pollution: No.

THE FACILITIES
Loos: 1U. **Showers** (outdoor 'bush' shower): 1U (free).
Other facilities: Washing-up area, campers' shelter, picnic table, chimenea, eggs and veg (in season) for sale, a gorgeous mountain hut-style hostel.
Stuff for children: 2 swings, 2 hammocks, red squirrel feeding station, a bit of duck feeding on request. **Recycling**: Everything.

THE RULES
Dogs: No dogs. **Fires**: In chimenea only; BBQs off grass (stands available).
Other: Don't disturb the lazy ducks.

PUB LIFE
The Old Bridge Inn (free house), Aviemore (11½ miles) – cosy fire and outdoor punters; open Mon–Thur 11am–midnight, Fri & Sat till 1am, Sun 12.30–midnight; food served 12–3pm & 6–9pm 7D (Fri & Sat till 10pm); 01479 811137; www.oldbridgeinn.co.uk.

SHOP
Nethy Bridge Village Store (Spar; 1 mile) – comprehensively stocked convenience store and PO; Mon–Sat 8am–6pm, Sun 9am–6pm; 01479 821217.

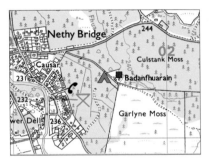

THERE AND AWAY
Train station: Carrbridge or Aviemore (10/12 miles) – Perth to Inverness line. Bus nos. 15, 34 and 209 (www.stagecoachbus.com) run to Nethy Bridge from Aviemore.

OUT AND ABOUT
Speyside Way – the 65-mile path from Buckie, on the Moray Firth, to Aviemore passes through Nethy Bridge (1 mile); 01340 881266; www.speysideway.org. The local area is also criss-crossed with footpaths for shorter wanders; www.exploreabernethy.co.uk.
National Cycle Route No. 7 (Inverness–Sunderland) passes through Boat of Garten (5½ miles) and is joined by numerous other local on-road and off-road cycle trails; www.sustrans.org.uk.
Landmark, Carrbridge (10 miles) – rock climbing, flume rides, treetop walk and some educational stuff craftily dressed up as fun; April to October/November to March adult £12.60/£4.10, child £10.50/£3.05; open daily 10am–5/6/7pm (depending on month); www.landmarkpark.co.uk.

open	Mid April to mid October
tiny campsites' rating	★ ★ ★
friendliness	☺ ☺ ☺
cost	BP ££, Couple £££, Family £££££

There are some campsites that you arrive at and immediately think, 'Ah yes, this is how it should be done.' The Lazy Duck is just such a one. From its hammocks strung across trees to its butterfly-filled wild-flower garden, it could hardly be more relaxed or aesthetically pleasing if it tried.

Just outside the village of Nethy Bridge, on the edge of the Cairngorms, and half a mile up a forest track, Lazy Duck's campsite is in a small glade guarded by a brigade of red squirrels and equipped with a chiminea and log seats for communal evening gatherings (for the campers; not the squirrels). Only four small tents are allowed on the site, so do check on the website for availability before you email to book.

The list of attractive features at the Lazy Duck is a long one and includes the bush shower (commune with nature the Australian way); the open-ended campers' shelter with its tea-light lanterns on the tables; the walk out to the juniper moor to view CairnGorm mountain; and the numerous eponymous, exotic and, it has to be said, lazy ducks.

Just to top it off, if you arrive by bicycle or on foot the owners not only guarantee to fit you in somewhere (if you haven't booked and the campsite's full), but you'll be greeted in the traditional Moroccan manner: with a mixture of green and home-grown fresh mint tea from a Berber teapot and dates from their own stock absolutely free. Fab.

Croft Road
Lochcarron
Ross-shire
IV54 8YA

Iain Macrae
01520 722898
dunrovinjo@tiscali.co.uk
Landranger: 24/25 (NG 906 400)

THE BASICS
Size: ½ acre.
Pitches: 21 (6 hardstanding).
Terrain: Flat terraces.
Shelter: Yes.
View: Loch Carron.
Waterside: A minute's walk from the shore.
Electric hook-ups: 6.
Noise/Light/Olfactory pollution: No.

THE FACILITIES
Loos: 2U. **Showers**: 2U (free).
Other facilities: Washing-up area, washing machine (£1.50), Lindy's Laundry in Lochcarron can dry clothes if it's raining; NB there is no CDP.
Stuff for children: No.
Recycling: Glass, tins, paper.

THE RULES
Dogs: Yes, under control. **Fires**: No open fires; BBQs off grass. **Other**: No.

PUB LIFE
The Rockvilla, Lochcarron (100 metres) – has a licensed restaurant (April to October 5–9pm 7D) but, sadly, no longer a public bar; 01520 722379; www.therockvilla.com. Try the similarly genteel **Lochcarron Hotel** for a bar and a later night; open 11am–'late' 7D; food served 12–8.45pm 7D; 01520 722226; www.lochcarronhotel.com.

SHOP
Lochcarron Food Centre (Spar and PO; ¼ mile) – multi-award-winning (rejoice!) large convenience store and off licence; open Mon–Fri 8am–7pm, Sat 8.30am–7pm, Sun 10am–4pm (shorter hours in winter); 01520 722209.

THERE AND AWAY
Train station: Strathcarron (3 miles) – Inverness to Kyle of Lochalsh line. DMK's bus no. 702 runs from Strathcarron to Lochcarron, or hop in a taxi (Lochcarron Taxis; 07774 499767).

OUT AND ABOUT
Strome Castle, Stromemore (3½ miles) – the romantic lochside ruins of a 15th-century stronghold (captured and unceremoniously blown up by the Mackenzies of Kintail in 1602), with splendid views down Loch Carron; free; always open; bit.ly/qmEiIP.
Attadale Gardens, nr Strathcarron (4¾ miles) – 20 acres of gardens created by Baron Schroder in the 19th century and completely reworked by artist Nicky Macpherson, with terrific views out to Skye; adult £4.50, child £1; open April to October Mon–Sat 10am–5.30pm; 01520 722603; www.attadalegardens.com.
Plockton (18 miles) – a remarkably pretty village at the far end of the loch and the setting for cult television series *Hamish MacBeth*; www.plockton.com.

ROSS-SHIRE

open	Early April to October
tiny campsites' rating	★ ★
friendliness	☺ ☺
cost	BP £, Couple ££, Family £££

Highland wind, as any Highlander will tell you, is just, well, faster than any wind anywhere else in Britain. Therefore, should you come around the eastern tip of the tidal Loch Carron and be suddenly hit by a piledriver of a gale that sparks visions of having your tent/campervan/caravan unceremoniously picked up and dumped in the loch; then there's good news: the Wee Camp Site is sheltered by such a stout barrier of fir trees along its western edge that peace and tranquillity are pretty much guaranteed here.

Perched up on a slope above Lochcarron village, the site has been made possible by the creation of terraces, each large enough for four or five pitches; with the upper ones enjoying a glorious view over the loch to Ben Killilan, Sguman Coinntich (snow-capped for much of the year), copious waterfalls and the mountains of the Killilan Forest. This rather steals the glory from the vista to the rear – Glas Bheinn and other mountains beyond – which most campsite owners would kill to possess. The soil on the terraces is rather thin, but there are some stones underneath the trees to aid and abet with anchoring tent pegs (and you might even find some alpine strawberries while you're fetching them).

Lochcarron, a village spun out as thin as silk along the lochside, has a surprising number of shops and services for its size including a good café, a bistro and even a bank. It also boasts a dozen local Munros and some excellent walking country (a book of routes is available at the tourist information centre).

Croft 9
Badrallach
Dundonnell
Ross-shire
IV23 2QP

Mick and Ali Stott
01854 633281
mail@badrallach.com
www.badrallach.com
Landranger: 19 (NH 066 917)

THE BASICS
Size: ⅘ acre.
Pitches: 19 (0 hardstanding).
Terrain: Mainly gently sloping.
Shelter: Some pitches.
View: Mountains, waterfalls and sea loch.
Waterside: Little Loch Broom (300 metres to the shore via a footpath).
Electric hook-ups: 3.
Noise/Light/Olfactory pollution: Lights on around bothy for late-night loo trips.

THE FACILITIES
Loos: 2M 2W 1D. **Showers**: 2U (free).
Other facilities: Kitchen, table-tennis table. If not booked by a group, the bothy facilities can be used by campers: dining area, peat-burning stove, darts, board games, tourist info, small library and flash settee; holiday cottage for rent; Eriba and Airstream caravans for hire; NB no CDP.
Stuff for children: No.
Recycling: No.

THE RULES
Dogs: If well behaved (sheep in adjacent fields). **Fires**: Firepits on half of pitches; BBQs off grass.
Other: Only 3 campervans or caravans on site at any one time, prior booking is essential.

PUB LIFE
Dundonnell Hotel (free house), nr Dundonnell (7½ miles) – choose either the Broombeg or the Soft Option Bar (and remind yourself that it's a very long walk to the nearest proper pub); open Mon–Sat 12–11pm, Sun till 10.30pm; food served 12–2pm 7D & Mon–Thur 6–8.30pm, Fri &

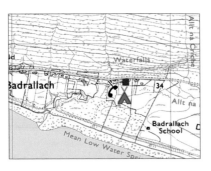

Sat till 9pm, Sun till 8pm; 01854 633204; www.dundonnellhotel.com.

SHOP
Dundonnell PO, nr Badcaul (14 miles) – well-stocked grocery; open Mon–Sat 8am–6pm; 01854 633208.

THERE AND AWAY
Train station: Garve (38 miles) – Inverness to Kyle of Lochalsh line. See facing page for onward transport options.

OUT AND ABOUT
An Teallach (8 miles) – 'Scotland's finest ridge walk', includes 2 Munros; 635-metre Beinn Ghobhlach (bit.ly/nHf29f) is just behind the campsite; and there's a beautiful 5-mile lochside stroll into the road-less off-grid community of Scoraig.
Gairloch Marine Life Centre (40 miles) – join an expert marine biologist on a 2-hour cruise to spot porpoises, whales, dolphins and basking sharks; adult £20, U18 £10; Easter to September trips at 10am, 12.30 & 3pm; www.porpoise-gairloch.co.uk.

open	All year
tiny campsites' rating	★ ★ ★
friendliness	☺ ☺ ☺
cost	BP ££, Couple ££, Family ££££

In a satisfyingly remote spot on the Scoraig Peninsula, with a most spectacular view – the ridge of An Teallach on the far side of Little Loch Broom dwarfing the few white houses beneath it – Badrallach offers campers the choice of a pitch in a small open field sloping towards the loch or one of a handful hidden away in the gorse. Your neighbours may include pine martens, red deer, golden eagles, white-tailed sea eagles and red squirrels; so keep your eyes peeled.

If you fancy an active stay, there's a fantastic range of equipment for hire from the site at very reasonable rates, including mountain bikes, a blo-kart (a three-wheeled sail board), a power kite (basically a kite far larger than nature intended), a tandem kayak, two single kayaks, an inflatable 6 h.p.-boat and even a Shetland whilly (a wooden clinker built sail boat).

The nearest shop is a hilly 14 miles away, but milk, bread and organic fruit and veg (in season) can be bought on site, while other inhabitants of the township will also happily supply free-range eggs and a wider range of your five-a-day. Furthermore, the owners run a collection service for the cost of the fuel and a tip' from Ullapool, Garve or Inverness. Alternatively, you can catch bus no. 804 (once daily in summer; www.decoaches.co.uk) from Inverness to within seven miles of the campsite and get picked up from there.

Throw into the mix a wonderfully well-turned-out gaslit bothy to hide in should the weather turn, and you've got a truly exceptional campsite.

Inver Caravan Park
Houstry Road
Dunbeath
Caithness
KW6 6EH

Rhona Gwillim

01593 731441

rhonagwillim@yahoo.co.uk

www.inver-caravan-park.co.uk

OS Landranger: 11/17 (ND 166 299)

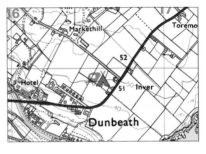

THE BASICS
Size: 1 acre.
Pitches: 17 (9 hardstanding).
Terrain: Gradual slope.
Shelter: Partial and not from east.
View: The North Sea (through the trees) and Dunbeath Castle.
Waterside: The sea is a field away, across the road.
Electric hook-ups: 17.
Noise/Light/Olfactory pollution: Some traffic on the A9.

THE FACILITIES
Loos: 1U. **Showers**: 3U (one of which is equipped for those with disabilities; free). **Other facilities**: Washing machine (£3), drying room, 70-metre washing line; washing-up area; wi-fi (£2.50/night or £5/week), B&B (3 rooms).
Stuff for children: No.
Recycling: Everything (inc. compost).

THE RULES
Dogs: Under control.
Fires: No open fires; BBQs off grass (stones on site).
Other: No.

PUB LIFE
The Inver Arms, a minute's walk down the A9, used to be one of the least attractive buildings in Scotland, with décor to match. Happily, it was taken over in late 2008 and was given a complete overhaul including a new name, the **Bay Owl** (free house), and now booking is essential; open 11am–midnight 7D; food served Mon–Fri 12–2.30pm & 5–9pm; Sat 12–3pm & 5–9pm, Sun 12.30–3pm & 5–8pm; 01593 731356.

SHOP
P & N (Spar), Dunbeath (½ mile) – small convenience store; open Mon–Wed 7.15am–6pm, Thur–Sat till 7pm, Sun 8.45am–5pm; 01593 731217.

THERE AND AWAY
Train station: Helmsdale (16 miles) – Inverness to Wick/Thurso line. From Helmsdale bus no. X99 (www.stagecoachbus.com) stops at Dunbeath.

OUT AND ABOUT
Dunbeath Heritage Centre (¾ mile) – an absorbing exploration of the history of this small village, from ancient rune-inscribed stones to present-day matters; adult £2, child free; open April to September Sun–Fri 10am–5pm, October to March Mon–Fri 11am–3pm; 01593 731233; www.dunbeath-heritage.org.uk.
Dunbeath Strath and Broch, Dunbeath (½ mile to start of walk) – stride along Dunbeath Water up to a 2,000-year-old Broch (tower), a high gorge and standing stones; free; always open; www.dunbeath-heritage.org.uk/trail.html.

open	All year
tiny campsites' rating	★ ★
friendliness	☺ ☺ ☺
cost	BP ££, Couple £££, Family ££££

High on a hill above the village of Dunbeath, this site looks out to the sea with one eye, and inland towards hills and mountains with the other.

It should be said straight off that the campsite is located slap-bang on the A9 as it cruises towards Thurso in the far north-east, but traffic around here is a whole lot sparser than that experienced further south, and at night becomes so light as to be almost unnoticeable. Indeed, you're more likely to be woken by the early morning calls of curlews than by anything speeding north. Facilities-wise, the loo and showers have undergone a complete refurbishment and now, aside from being all shiny and new, boast underfloor heating too.

Just 38 miles short of John o'Groats, the site is very handy for a last or first night on the End-to-End route, as well as for trips to the Orkneys from Scrabster (28 miles), or a visit to Whaligoe Steps (13 miles) for a look at Britain's oddest harbour (it has always been laughably dangerous).

Despite its self-designation as a caravan park, this site is just as welcoming to campers as caravanners, and the former have the pick of the best pitches up at the top end of the field. Though not as astonishingly cheap as it once was for backpackers and cyclists, it's still one of the best value campsites for walkers and riders in Scotland. Furthermore, anyone staying for a week gets the seventh night free. Result!

74 Halladale Inn

Melvich
Sutherland
KW14 7YJ

Ian and Marilyn Fling
01641 531282
info@halladaleinn.co.uk
www.halladaleinn.co.uk
Landranger: 10 (NC 887 640)

THE BASICS
Size: 9/10 acre.
Pitches: 19 (11 hardstanding).
Terrain: Gently sloping.
Shelter: Some pitches in lee of pub.
View: Fields, the valley of the River Halladale and the North Sea.
Waterside: A 10-minute walk to the beach.
Electric hook-ups: 11.
Noise/Light/Olfactory pollution: Music from the pub goes on until late; streetlights at night.

THE FACILITIES
Loos: 1M 2W. **Showers**: 1M 1W (free).
Other facilities: Washing-up area, washing machine, tumble-dryer, 2 picnic tables.
Stuff for children: No.
Recycling: No.

THE RULES
Dogs: Yes.
Fires: No open fires; BBQ provided (it's an oil drum sliced in half). **Other**: No.

PUB LIFE
Halladale Inn (free house) – the popular restaurant specialises in locally sourced food; open Mon–Thur 11am–11pm, Fri 11–1am, Sat till midnight, Sun 12–11pm; food served 12–8pm 7D.

SHOP
The West End PO, Portskerra (1¼ miles) – basic foodstuffs, newspapers & off licence; open Mon–Sat 9am–6pm; 01641 531219.

THERE AND AWAY
Train station: Forsinard (15 miles) – Inverness to Wick/Thurso line. Take a

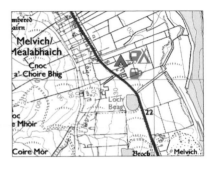

taxi from the station as public transport options are few and far between.

OUT AND ABOUT
Strathnaver Museum, Bettyhill (14 miles) – housed in the former church of St Columba, the museum takes visitors on a tour, from Strathnaver's numinous past all the way to the Highland Clearances; adult £2, child 50p, U5 free; open April to October Mon–Sat 10am–5pm; 01641 521418; www.strathnavermuseum.org.uk.
Forsinard Nature Reserve (13 miles) – wet bogs aren't, perhaps, humankind's favourite terrain, but there's plenty of wildlife that won't give them the cold shoulder. At Forsinard there's a chance of spying greenshanks, hen harriers, golden plovers, dunlin and the odd golden eagle; otters in the river or bog pools; and herds of red deer; free; open daily April to October 9am–6pm; 01955 602596; bit.ly/pSjrQa.

open	All year
tiny campsites' rating	★ ★
friendliness	☺ ☺
cost	BP £, Couple ££, Family ££££

There can be few campsites in Britain that are more happily situated than this one next to Melvich's Halladale Inn on the not-quite-as-wild-as-you-might imagine north coast of Scotland. Virtually all the pitches here enjoy views of sheep-filled fields that tumble down to the River Halladale as it makes its final lurch into the sea.

Campervanners and caravanners will enjoy the site's fast-draining gravelly section, while campers will be pleased to get onto the grass beyond to savour the view. The facilities are clean and welcoming and the pub is not only open all day, but serves food for eight straight hours of it.

The beach at Halladale Bay – a 10-minute walk down through those same sheep-filled fields – is simply captivating. Perhaps it's due to the sand dunes that pile up behind the beach, or it could be the oystercatchers, ringed plovers and curlews that flit past and up the clear shallow river, while cuckoos and wood pigeons lend their calls to the aural backdrop. You know you're only a hop and a step from a pub and the coastal road and civilisation and everything, but it does really feel like you've entered some enchanted seaside wilderness, which is perhaps why it also appeals to surfers (well, that and the waves, probably).

If you feel a need to seek out pleasures further afield, Orkney can be reached from Scrabster (16 miles) by ferry, while the little village of Tongue (26 miles) and its ruined castle are also worth a visit.

North Shawbost
Isle of Lewis
HS2 0BQ

- Iain Macaulay
- 01851 710504
- eileanfraoich@btinternet.com
- eileanfraoich.co.uk
- OS Landranger: 8/13 (NB 256 463)

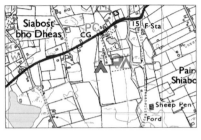

THE BASICS
Size: 7/10 acre.
Pitches: 25 (12 hardstanding).
Terrain: Flat.
Shelter: Some protection from southerly winds.
View: A glimpse of sea through the trees.
Waterside: No.
Electric hook-ups: 12.
Noise/Light/Olfactory pollution: Exterior lights on buildings.

THE FACILITIES
Loos: 2M 2W 1D. **Showers**: 1M 1W 1D (20p for '2 min.').
Other facilities: Kitchen (inc. washing-up area, gas hob, fridge and toaster), dining area, laundry taken in, payphone, hairdryer, CDP.
Stuff for children: There's a playing field right next door with a football pitch, and for budding Olympians a long-jump pit and a shot-put circle (shots not provided). The village school's swimming pool is also open to non-pupils (01851 710212).
Recycling: Glass, bottles, tins, organic waste.

THE RULES
Dogs: On leads; an exercise area is provided. **Fires**: No open fires; bricks available for BBQs off grass.
Other: In order not to upset local people, no washing is to be hung out on a Sunday.

PUB LIFE
The Doune Braes Hotel (free house), Carloway (7 miles) – fairly standard hotel bar with restaurant, but in a terrifically scenic location; open Mon–Thur 12–11pm,

Fri–Sat till midnight, Sun 12.30–9pm; food served Mon–Sat 12–8.30pm, Sun 12.30–7.30pm; 01851 643252.

SHOP
The **Welcome Inn Filling Station**, Barvas (7 miles) – basic foodstuffs & various takeaways; open Mon–Fri 7am–10pm, Sat 8am–10pm; 01851 840343.

THERE AND AWAY
Ferry Terminal: Stornoway (19 miles) – Caledonian MacBrayne ferries (www.calmac.co.uk) to/from Ullapool. Bus no. W2 from Stornoway stops in Shawbost.

OUT AND ABOUT
Shawbost Museum (200 metres) – a look at local life down the ages; open April to September Mon–Fri ('usually') 2–5pm; 01851 710710.
The Black House, Arnol (7½ miles) – a traditional Lewis thatched house kept exactly as it was when abandoned in 1966, along with a furnished 1920s white house; adult £4, child £2.40; open April to September Mon–Sat 9.30am–5.30pm (see website for other months); bit.ly/nJ2QRr.

open	May to October
tiny campsites' rating	★ ★
friendliness	☺ ☺
cost	BP £, Couple £££, Family £££

If prizes were awarded for sprawling, the village of Shawbost ('Shlaboist' in Gaelic) would never have to worry about owning an empty trophy-cabinet. Its houses straddle the coast road so interminably that anyone approaching Eilean Fraoich from the north could be forgiven for imagining that they might never arrive.

If and when they do, they will discover a campsite that is very far removed from the rough and rugged Lewisian landscape that surrounds it. At Eilean Fraoich, tent pegs slide into an immaculately kept lawn beside a neat, modern bungalow. Meanwhile, a recent extension has added nine extra hardstanding pitches. The facilities are spotless, and the kitchen and dining room are not only welcome (since it can get very breezy here indeed), but are so café-like that when you bustle about preparing your dinner you can have fun pretending you're a chef who has just opened up an exclusive Hebridean eatery, if you like.

Milk and gas, that ever-winning combination, can be purchased on site, as can newspapers if ordered the day before, which is a rare luxury. In cold weather, the owner will even supply blankets on request.

The tariff is based on tent size rather than the number of people in it, so if you can shoehorn your family/friends into a two-man job, so much the better. The sea is but a quarter of a mile away, although the nearest access to it requires a 20-minute stroll, during which you can all get some feeling back into your limbs.

A Word for Walkers

There's something pleasingly visceral about backpacking. It's just you, the outdoors, a few victuals and a simple shelter for the night. No matter that your provisions are a vacuum-packed bag of dehydrated vegetable curry and that your shelter sports the latest developments in ultra-lightweight rip-stop trilaminate; there's still an element of being at one with nature that is hard to beat.

Furthermore, campsite owners love walkers. Maybe they sense that this is somehow 'as it ought to be', or perhaps they just like the fact that walkers have no vehicles that may need towing off the field if it pours with rain. Whatever the reason, time and time again I've been told by campsite owners, 'We don't turn away hikers, no matter how full we might be – we always find a corner for them somewhere.' One proprietor informed me that she'd even had walkers staying in her garden when her camping field was full. That's not to say that it's advisable to rock up anywhere and hope, of course, but it's nice to know that there are plenty of people out there who will take pity on you if you happen to wander in on spec, blistered and hunchbacked from a long day's hike.

One of my favourite long-distance footpaths is the South Downs Way, the route across the chalky hills that bounce from Winchester down to Eastbourne. Gumber Farm (p64) in Sussex is not only handily placed for a night stop, but is even closer to the route of the Monarch's Way, the mammoth 615-mile path tracing Charles II's escape from England after the battle of Worcester in 1651. Since the farm was beloved of the writer Hilaire Belloc, it is perhaps appropriate that the West Sussex Literary Trail is also within striking distance.

Further west, anyone who spends a night or two at Porthllisky Farm (p134) and who doesn't feel an urgent desire to explore St David's Peninsula on foot should have their pulse checked at once to make sure their heart's still functioning. Meanwhile, the five-mile hike from Badrallach (p178) along Little Loch Broom to the isolated and road-less community at Scoraig (the locals simply get around by boat) is one guaranteed to enthuse even the most reluctant of walkers.

While all the campsites in this book make splendid bases for a day's wandering about, there are some that offer the added bonus of lying close to, or right on, a long-distance footpath. Thus, for those planning a longer walk, here's a list of signed trails near featured campsites:

Trail	No.	Campsite
Beacons Way	54	Llanddeusant
Brenig Way	62	Buzzard Rock Camping Club
Cambrian Way	54	Llanddeusant
	60	Ty'n Cornel
Cleveland Way	46	Park Farm
Cumbria Way	41	Birchbank Farm
Cumbrian Coastal Way	41	Birchbank Farm
Fen Rivers Way	30	Braham Farm
Hadrian's Wall Path	50	Quarryside
Monarch's Way	20	Gumber Farm
Mortimer Trail	34	The Buzzards
Norfolk Coast Path	29	Scaldbeck Cottage
Offa's Dyke Path	61	Ty Maen
Ouse Valley Way	30	Braham Farm
Pembrokeshire Coast Path	51	Porthllisky Farm
Pennine Way	47	Highside Farm
Severn Way	13	Rectory Farm
South Downs Way	20	Gumber Farm
South West Coast Path	1	Land's End
	2	Coverack
	3	Broad Meadow House
	4	Dennis Farm
	5	Scadghill Farm
	8	Millslade
	10	California Cottage
Southern Upland Way	66	The Ken Bridge Hotel
Speyside Way	70	The Lazy Duck
Sussex Border Path	21	Evergreen Farm Woodland
Thames Path	17	Rushey Lock
	18	Pinkhill Lock
	19	Cookham Lock
West Sussex Literary Trail	20	Gumber Farm
Wye Valley Walk	57	Radnors End
	58	Trericket Mill
Wysis Way	14	Daneway Inn

A Word for Cyclists

There's very little to compare in this life with the sensation of having an open road before you, a bicycle beneath whose pedals whirr round at the slightest pressure and a friendly wind at your back. All you need to add is a jaunty whistle, a couple of panniers and a tiny tent, and the world is yours.

As mentioned elsewhere, I visited all 75 campsites in this book by bicycle – an old-school Falcon Oxford tourer I bought second-hand 12 years ago for the princely sum of £28 – and can thus confirm not only that they are accessible on two wheels, but that getting to them can be an immensely pleasurable business, especially if you let the train do most of the work first (see Taking the Train, p190).

I felt, therefore, that I'd take the liberty of passing on a few insider tips to any who fancy visiting some of the campsites in this book *à bicyclette*.

For the novice or occasional cyclist

If you're the sort of cyclist who is not naturally wedded to the saddle, it's always a good idea to have a quick peek at a map to see if your campsite of choice is surrounded by contours. Cycling 20 miles on the flat of the Fens is a very different matter to pedalling the same distance in humpy-bumpy Devon. I once made the mistake of taking my girlfriend, who was brought up in ironing-board flat Cambridgeshire, for a ride in Northumberland that I had assumed would be fairly straightforward and take us no longer than 90 minutes. When we arrived at our destination four hours later after some killer hills I had lost a considerable number of hard-won boyfriend points.

So, if you were to cycle to Sweet Meadows (p34), you would be advised not to start off from Exeter, as there's an almighty hill between the two. However, Yeoford station, a little to the north-west, lends itself to a route via far more manageable ascents. Likewise, head for Millslade (p36) via Lynmouth and you will encounter the thigh-punishing Countisbury Hill, which starts off at a gradient of 1:4 and doesn't get much easier for the next two miles.

If even the prospect of a gentle incline brings you out in a cold sweat, there is still hope – just book yourself in to any of the East Anglian sites (see pp76–87) and breeze on in.

For more experienced cyclists

The more practised cyclists among you will no doubt be chafing at such advice and are probably even now making a mental note to approach Millslade via Lynmouth just for the sheer joy of taking on a hill worthy of the name. If you find yourself in this category, allow me to recommend Gwersyll Maes-y-Bryn (p158), a three-mile climb from Llanrwst, and Badrallach (p178), one of the remotest sites in the country and one with a real sense of destination, especially when you look down on it from the top of the final hill and realise that all there is between you and it is a long, exhilarating drop.

Something for everyone

You'll find a Cyclists' category on p17 listing all the campsites that are either located in countryside that cries out to be cycled through or are close to designated trails. To get you started, here are the cycle paths and mountain bike circuits that are easily accessible from campsites in this book:

Black and White Trail	34	The Buzzards
Brenig Trail	62	Buzzard Rock Camping Club
C2C	48	The Old Vicarage
Camel Trail	4	Dennis Farm
Deers Leap Park mountain bike trails	21	Evergreen Farm Woodland
Forest of Bowland cycle routes	39	Crawshaw Farm
Glastonbury & Wells National Byway Loop	9	Bridge Farm
Hadrian's Cycleway	50	Quarryside
Holderness National Byway Loop	44	Elmtree Farm
Kennet and Avon Canal cycle path	12	Church Farm
Killer Loop mountain bike circuit	56	The Castle Inn
National Cycle Route No. 7	70	The Lazy Duck
Seven Stanes mountain bike trails	66	The Ken Bridge Hotel
	67	Glenmidge Smithy
Water Rail Way	31	The Bubble Car Museum
Way of the Roses	43	Jelley Legs
West Loch Lomond cycle path	69	Inchcailloch

Taking the Train

One of the many joys of camping is that it allows us to wave a fond farewell to the trappings of everyday modern life. For a brief period we allow ourselves a respite from work, television, central heating, emails and, if we enter into the spirit of things, mobile phones too. It can also be very satisfying to forego the stress and bother of driving to a chosen holiday destination in favour of getting there by public transport.

Contrary to popular opinion, the railway system in Britain is pretty efficient – in the months I spent roving around the country researching this book, I didn't experience a single cancellation and, miraculously, the only time a train was really late coincided with the one occasion on which I'd misjudged the distance from a campsite to a station and got in horribly late too.

I took my bike on the train wherever I went but, if you're not a cyclist, the vast majority of the campsites can still be reached from their nearest station by bus or, in some cases, simply by walking (see Easy Public Transport, p19). Planning the journey is also now a lot simpler and more straightforward with the advent of such websites as Transport Direct (www.transportdirect.info).

However, it must be admitted that the proliferation of train companies that criss-cross the nation nowadays is apt to cause a certain amount of confusion. Therefore, to help make things a bit clearer, there follows a brief guide to the rail companies that serve the campsites featured in this book.

ARRIVA TRAINS WALES
Network: ATW covers the whole of Wales and has lines reaching out from the principality to Manchester, Birmingham and Cheltenham. The Explore Wales Pass allows passengers to travel over the entire ATW network, the Ffestiniog and Welsh Highland railways and most scheduled bus services.
Website: www.arrivatrainswales.co.uk
Ticket sales: 08709 000773 (Welsh Language service: 08456 040500)

CROSS COUNTRY
Network: A main line running from Cornwall to Aberdeen with routes off to Manchester, Reading, Cambridge and Bournemouth.
Website: www.crosscountrytrains.co.uk
Ticket sales: 08448 110124

EAST COAST
Network: Stretching up the spine of Britain from London King's Cross to the East Midlands, Yorkshire and

Humberside, north-east England and Scotland all the way north to Aberdeen and Inverness.
Website: www.eastcoast.co.uk
Ticket sales: 08457 225225

EAST MIDLANDS TRAINS
Network: An extensive service radiating out from Nottingham to take in London, Leicester, Crewe, Matlock, Liverpool, Sheffield, York, Skegness and Norwich among others.
Website: www.eastmidlandstrains.co.uk
Ticket sales: 08457 125678

FIRST GREAT WESTERN
Network: Includes south Wales, the West Country to the far end of Cornwall, the Cotswolds, and large parts of Southern England, with frequent services to and from London.
Website: www.firstgreatwestern.co.uk
Ticket sales: 08457 000125

NATIONAL EXPRESS EAST ANGLIA
Network: Covers Cambridgeshire, Norfolk, Suffolk, much of Essex and some of Hertfordshire, with trains leaving from London.
Website: www.nationalexpresseastanglia.com
Ticket sales: 08456 007245

NORTHERN
Network: Spreads over the whole of northern England from Crewe, Stoke, Buxton and Nottingham in the south, to Carlisle and Newcastle in the north.
Website: www.northernrail.org
Ticket sales: 08442 413454

SCOTRAIL
Network: ScotRail runs trains on all Scottish routes and boasts a sleeper service linking London with northern Scotland.
Website: www.scotrail.co.uk
Ticket sales: 08457 550033

SOUTH WEST TRAINS
Network: From London to Portsmouth, Weymouth, Exeter, Reading and the Isle of Wight.
Website: www.southwesttrains.co.uk
Ticket sales: 08456 000650

SOUTHERN
Network: Covers the counties to the south of London including Surrey, East and West Sussex, along with some of Kent and Hampshire.
Website: www.southernrailway.com
Ticket sales: 08451 272920

TRANSPENNINE EXPRESS
Network: As the name suggests, TE covers routes across the Pennines from Liverpool, Blackpool and Barrow across to Hull, Cleethorpes and Scarborough. They also run services up the east coast to Newcastle and the west coast to Glasgow and Edinburgh.
Website: www.tpexpress.co.uk (check out the bouncing rabbits on the interactive network map)
Ticket sales: 0871 000125

VIRGIN TRAINS
Network: From London Euston, the Virgin empire extends largely north-west to the West Midlands, the north Welsh coast, Cheshire, Manchester, Liverpool, Carlisle and up to Glasgow and Edinburgh.
Website: www.virgintrains.co.uk
Ticket sales: 08719 774222

USEFUL INFO
National Rail Enquires: 08457 484950 (24 hours); www.nationalrail.co.uk.

A to B Magazine's Bike/Rail Page is full of excellent information on when and where you can travel on trains, buses and ferries with a bicycle: www.atob.org.uk/Bike_Rail_2.html.

AUTHOR ACKNOWLEDGEMENTS

I'd like to proffer my heartfelt thanks to all those who helped make my life sweeter in some way or other during the research for this book, and in particular: Rensie and Damian 'bassman' Basher; Deb, Sam and Jethro Best; Robert Stanford; Henrietta Evans; Cecilia at Pandy; James Bladen and Vanna Lundin; Julie and Chris Hindley; the van Zijl family; Ros Loten; Carey and Dave Watson; Chloë and Kate; Warren and Denhy for their fab mango and chilli salad; Sara and Estelle with their slightly less than fab incinerated marshmallows; Dave Dukes; Gail and Danny Freeman-Dinner; Elaine at The Buzzards; Thomas and June McMillan; Rin and Cobby, purveyors of the finest vegetarian jelly; Michael Breckon at The National Byway; Carl and Viv Palmer; Tara at Middle Ninfa; Ralph Smorgasbord; Kim, Nick, Freddy and Jet; Clive and Edwin; Jack Thurston, Les Roberts, Ellie Banks at First Great Western; Carla Rinaldi at ScotRail; John Gelson and Paul Williams at National Express East Coast; Carolyn Watson and Clare Conlin at Northern Rail; Chris Hudson at Southern Rail; Emma Knight at Southwest Trains and East Midland Trains; Maggie Abbett at Arriva Trains Wales; Ellen Rossiter at National Express East Anglia; David Mallender at Transpennine Express; Lee West at Cross Country; Tracy Clifton at Virgin Trains; Iain Crawford at Vango; Rob Cater at Decathlon; the staff at Bethnal Green library; The Guildensterns, and The Boys and Ellie and Apricot.

Special thanks to Elisabeth Whitebread for her help with research and for her general forbearance.

And, finally, I would like to express my gratitude to the scores of campsite owners who welcomed me warmly no matter which of my two highly attractive post-cycling states I arrived in: soaked to the skin or wreathed in sweat. It's very much appreciated.

For the record, the tents I use are a Quechua T2 ultralight pro, Vango's Helium 100 and, increasingly nowadays, a Vaude Power Lizard. The T2 is a doddle to pitch, is very roomy inside and, for a light tent, is very cheap. The Helium finds its way into my rucksack when I need something really small and light – it's the same weight as a bag of sugar and folds away into almost nothing. And for sheer luxury (the porch is huge) combined with terrifically light weight (again, it's just a kilo), I travel with the Power Lizard. Every home should have one.

Lastly, for those who take pleasure in finding out such things, the vast majority of the photographs in this book were taken on a Fuji F200EXR. More recent ones were snapped with a Nikon D3000.

Tiny Campsites
Researched, written and photographed by:
Dixe Wills
Publisher: Jonathan Knight
Managing Editor: Sophie Dawson
Design: Dave Jones
Cover Design & Artwork: Harriet Yeomans
Proofreaders: Claire Wedderburn-Maxwell, Nikki Sims
Marketing: Shelley Bowdler

Published by: Punk Publishing, 3 The Yard, Pegasus Place, London SE11 5SD
Distributed by: Portfolio Books, 2nd Floor, Westminster House, Kew Road, Richmond, Surrey TW9 2ND

All photographs © Dixe Wills except the following (all reproduced with permission): p5 left © Mick Stott/Badrallach; front cover flap & pages 20, 40, 60, 76, 88, 104, 132 & 164 © Andy Stothert; p5 right & 151 © Sophie Dawson; p45 © Paul Cooper; p53 © Will Chester-Master; p116 © Dave Jelley/Jelley Legs; p181 © Colette & Christian Gobeil; p185 © Iain Macaulay/Eilean Fraoich. Cover © Harriet Yeomans.

OS Maps created by Lovell Johns Limited. Based upon Ordnance Survey digital map data © Crown Copyright 2011 Licence Number 43368U.

Punk Publishing takes its environmental responsibilities seriously. This book has been printed on paper made from renewable sources and we continue to work with our printers to reduce our overall environmental impact.

We hope you've enjoyed reading *Tiny Campsites* and that it's inspired you to explore Britain's best littlest sites. Those featured are a personal selection chosen by the author. Dixe Wills visited hundreds of campsites to find this selection, but it hasn't been possible for him to visit every British campsite. So, if you know of a special place that's an acre or under that you think should be included, please send an email to tinycampsites@punkpublishing.co.uk telling us the name and location of the campsite, some contact details and why it's so special. We'll credit all useful contributions in the next edition, and senders of the best emails will receive a complimentary copy.